UMBERTO MARIANI

Living Masks:
The Achievement of
Pirandello

UNIVERSITY OF TORONTO PRESS
Toronto Buffalo London

© University of Toronto Press Incorporated 2008
Toronto Buffalo London
www.utppublishing.com
Printed in Canada

ISBN 978-0-8020-9899-3 (cloth)
ISBN 978-0-8020-9600-5 (paper)

Printed on acid-free paper

Toronto Italian Studies

Library and Archives Canada Cataloguing in Publication

Mariani, Umberto, 1927–
    Living masks : the achievement of Pirandello / Umberto Mariani.

(Toronto Italian studies)
Includes bibliographical references and index.
ISBN 978-0-8020-9899-3 (bound). – ISBN 978-0-8020-9600-5 (pbk.)

1. Pirandello, Luigi, 1867–1936 – Criticism and interpretation.
I. Title.   II. Series.

PQ4835.I7Z6715 2008   852′.912   C2008-904386-3

University of Toronto Press acknowledges the financial assistance to its publishing program of the Canada Council for the Arts and the Ontario Arts Council.

University of Toronto Press acknowledges the financial support for its publishing activities of the Government of Canada through the Book Publishing Industry Development Program (BPIDP).

LIVING MASKS: THE ACHIEVEMENT OF PIRANDELLO

Th   s
un   n
cer   d
thr   -
en   n
su   i
pre   r
pla
l   f
Pir   d
tec   e
ref   n
on   e
di   -
ers   r
ap   o
ad   r
ori
   y
ma   ,
an
(T

UMBERTO MARIANI is a professor emeritus in the Department of Italian at Rutgers University.

The Nobel Prize-winning dramatist Luigi Pirandello (1867–1936) is considered one of the most innovative playwrights of the twentieth century and also one of the most complex. While his influence spread throughout modernist and postmodernist works, many first-time audiences and readers are confronted with the difficulty associated with such a radical aesthetic experience. In *Living Masks*, Umberto Mariani presents a clear and comprehensive introduction of Pirandello's major plays for general readers, students, and scholars new to Pirandello.

Functioning as a guide to understanding the fundamental themes of Pirandello's plays, the author also examines the critical, aesthetic, and textual problems associated with these plays. He provides extensive reflection on some of the failings of early and contemporary criticism of Pirandello's works and offers many corrections of interpretative direction that will be significant and helpful to directors and performers. In particular, Mariani presents a deeper understanding and greater appreciation of Pirandello's works as a challenge to the tendency to adapt and modify them, which drastically deprive the works of their original power and beauty.

A concise and accessible introduction to a twentieth-century literary master, *Living Masks* will be of interest to dramatists, literary scholars, and students and scholars of Italian studies.

Toronto Italian Studies

Contents

Preface

This work on the masterpieces of Pirandello's theatre was intended to serve a diverse group of readers, and thus to perform different functions. It can be read as an introductory essay to the major plays of Pirandello by general readers, or students, or scholars who, in their first approach to Pirandello, want to understand the fundamental themes of these plays, as well as the critical, technical, and aesthetic problems that were developed by and around them. Therefore, the number of footnotes has been limited to the absolutely indispensable, to avoid distracting the reader's attention; and the bibliography provided is an 'essential' one, to avoid overwhelming the reader with a bibliographical apparatus that has by now reached enormous proportions.

The scholar who is already fairly familiar with the Pirandellian theatre, on the other hand, should recognize that this study is aware throughout of the problems tied to these plays by past and recent criticism, a criticism so vast that a detailed annotation of it at every allusion would have required endless interruptions and digressions and numberless pages of footnotes. Yet the dialogue with some of Pirandello's critics attempted here becomes imperative when they continue, for instance, to see in *Liolà* a work steeped in the naturalism of Verga and Capuana; or are blind to the richness of both theme and form that makes *Henry IV* a masterpiece worthy of comparison with *Six Characters*; or misread as fundamental principles of Pirandello's poetics the pretentious rubbish ironically given to Dr Hinkfuss; or see the *meretrix magna* who generates and devours her children in the figure of La Spera of *La nuova colonia*; or attempt to close the enormous gap that separates the futurists from Pirandello. Nor could this study ignore the books on the Theatre of the Absurd or the works of Brecht that give not a word of recognition to Pirandello's profound influence.

Many of the readings proposed here and the discussion of various misreadings could also be of help to those who stage Pirandello's plays. It seems that the very directors who in recent decades have enjoyed the reputation of being most knowledgeable about Pirandello's theatre have most radically changed, adapted, and rewritten it, a process inconceivable to anyone who has really understood the thematic richness and the expressive power of the major plays. And not only Italian directors have taken that liberty. In the United States I have seen *Six Characters* stripped of the entire initial section during which the theatrical company's players are rehearsing *Il gioco delle parti* (a play frustratingly incomprehensible to them), as if it were a dispensable encumbrance instead of an essential part of the play; I have seen that *Gioco delle parti* replaced by a portion of a soap opera, that is, by today's television equivalent of what in a Pirandellian context would have been the sentimental bourgeois theatre – the very opposite of what *Il gioco delle parti* means to the clueless theatrical company the six Pirandellian characters have chanced upon. I have seen numerous adaptations of the other plays and never an integral Pirandellian text. During the year the fiftieth anniversary of Pirandello's death was celebrated, most American theatrical companies decided to 'honour' the greatest playwright of the twentieth century by performing at least one of his plays, yet not one of them used an integral text by Pirandello; all made use of 'adaptations.' This persistent choice, in either the United States or Italy, barely conceals the implication that Pirandello's great works need linguistic, stylistic, and structural 'improvement.'

It is hoped, then, that this book may also lead directors and actors to a better understanding of, and consequently a greater respect for, the texts of the masterpieces of a Pirandello who rarely missed the rehearsal of one of his plays, although he felt great pain if even the tone of voice of an actor was different from how he had imagined it should be, and once lamented to an interviewer: 'If you came to the rehearsal of one of my plays, you would realize what a torture, what a torment it is for me' (*Il tempo*, 9 March 1922).

Finally, the last chapter should at least briefly suggest the enormous influence Pirandello – and his dramatic masterpieces in particular – has had on the theatre, the literature, and indeed the culture of the entire twentieth century, an influence that has not yet ceased to be felt in the twenty-first.

Portions of the material that eventually flowed into this book were the subject of oral presentation at literary symposia and professional gatherings and found their way into print, all in more or less 'earlier' versions than their final form within the integral development of this book. Thus, an earlier version of the introductory chapter, the topic of a lecture given at Fordham and Bryn Mawr, was published in *Canadian Journal of Italian Studies*, 12, 38–9 (1989): 1–9; an earlier version of the chapter on *Liolà* was published in *Review of National Literatures*, 14 (1987): 31–46; an essay presented at a Pirandello symposium at Hofstra on *Six Characters* appeared (drastically shortened by the editor) in *A Companion to Pirandello Studies*, ed. John Di Gaetani (Westport, CT: Greenwood, 1991); an earlier Italian version of the chapter on *Henry IV*, following a lecture given at C.W. Post, appeared in *Rivista di studi pirandelliani*, 3, 6 (June–Sept. 1980): 5–13; another paper in Italian, on *Each in His Own Way*, presented at a convention of AAIS, appeared in its proceedings, *Italian Culture*, 8 (1990): 347–61. Finally, the topics of two papers presented at other professional gatherings and published in their proceedings became part of the final chapter: Pirandello's relationship, or non-relationship, with futurism, treated in a paper presented at a NEMLA convention (*NEMLA Italian Studies*, 10 [1986]: 71–84); and Pirandello's influence on the existentialist and absurdist theatre, treated in a paper presented at an AATI convention (*Italiana* [1988]: 225–69).

LIVING MASKS: THE ACHIEVEMENT OF PIRANDELLO

1 Introduction: The 'Pirandellian' Character

> He who has the good fortune to be born a live character can laugh even at death. He will never die!
>
> (*Six Characters*, I 58)[1]

In the structure of the most representative works of Pirandello, the major works of his maturity, a fundamental opposition recurs with increasing clarity between those characters who question or reject the values and conditions to which their society is determined to bind them – with its customs, its prejudices, its philistinism, its self-assurance, its claim to knowledge and superior wisdom – and the representatives and supporters of that society. This is the opposition through which the quintessential 'Pirandellian' character is revealed.

'Pirandellian' characters, thus, are those who, as silent victims or open rebels, are set in opposition to the bourgeois characters who are the functional embodiment of their society. The fact that the 'Pirandellian' characters too, for the most part, come from a bourgeois background does not at all diminish this fundamental opposition, but rather establishes its essentially ethical nature and structural function.

The Pirandellian character is necessarily one who suffers, enduring thereby a timeless existential condition, but also the particular condition of humanity in our time – perhaps one of the reasons for the vitality and modernity of Pirandello's work and particularly of his theatre. His characters have lost the comforting sense of stability and self-confidence of the bourgeois world of the end of the nineteenth century; they are assailed by doubts about their identity and the possibility of ever realizing or communicating it, of establishing a normal, functioning relationship with the society in which they find themselves; they have lost the sense of unity, of a community of thought and belief, and of faith in the means to communicate them that the late-nineteenth-century bourgeois world enjoyed; they suffer from their loss and protest dramatically against it.

As the old century came to its end and the new approached the catastrophe of the First World War, the bourgeoisie in Europe and particularly in Italy was progressively losing the dominant position it had enjoyed during the struggle for Italy's reunification and the period that followed. With the political trade-unionist mass movements of the proletariat on one side and the rise of the new industrial baronies on the other, the bourgeois intellectuals saw their own role becoming increasingly irrelevant. Yet that bourgeois world had once seemed so solid and secure, indeed so complacent in the principles and the institutions that ruled social behaviour; it had seemed especially confident in its positive faith in the omnipotence of scientific knowledge. Now instead those intellectuals felt betrayed. The promises of that security had not been kept: scientific 'positivism' had been unable to actually guarantee anything positive; moral convictions had often revealed themselves as hypocritical masks concealing under an apparent harmony a debased reality, a reality that was disintegrating, no longer sustained by the now empty forms of its false ideals – so different, on their utilitarian underside, from the heroic values of the first half of the century. It is this sense of betrayal that the Pirandellian characters express: they have discovered the meanness, the hypocrisy, the pretentiousness, the shabby values of petit bourgeois ideals.

Once the old, empty values and ideals have been perceived and rejected, it becomes impossible to hold on to the unified vision of reality that society had fostered; reality breaks down into a meaningless succession of events, which the representatives of the middle class, in their continuing claims to certainty and self-assurance, may still think they control, while the Pirandellian characters clearly grasp the fragmentation and decay of a reality that has lost all credibility.

And if historical reality in its intellectual, ethical, and social aspects breaks down, the certainties and assumptions regarding the individual as such, the integrity of the person, identity itself, cannot avoid collapse. The Pirandellian characters must experience not only the disintegration of the social reality amidst whose assurances they were raised, but also the disintegration of their own personality, of the comforting certainties regarding their identity, their personal worth; they must live what Pirandello in his illuminating preface to *Six Characters* calls the drama of 'life devoid of form' (I 44). The crisis of the structures of social life and of behaviour is reflected in the individual soul, which is unable to stay afloat following the shipwreck of the forms of objective, external, social reality. The Pirandellian characters proclaim the loss of their own form, of their unity, of the certainty of their knowledge and understanding of their own truth, and of its communicability; this is the condition at the root of the drama they bring with them on to the stage.

But they do not accept the loss of their form; they suffer from and protest against it as an unjust privation. They feel the need for that form, that consistency, that unity and self-assurance, for an existence supported by a system of values and ideals. They assert that need as a fundamentally human and insuppressible one: the need to know one's identity and to communicate what one is; the need to identify with, to integrate oneself into, a stable society, to enjoy its recognition, to find a sense of security in it. And they aspire to this tenaciously, as to a birthright.

From the exile of this 'life devoid of form' the Pirandellian characters long, then, for a form, and declare their need for an enduring structure, which, however, cannot be the reality that had shamefully disintegrated shortly before, the hypocritical forms of bourgeois behaviour, with their devalued content. They are not nostalgic reactionaries. To be different from the old one, the new form must possess an absolute, unassailable unity and solidity – that is, an impossible, unattainable unity and solidity. Indeed, the worst aspect of the outworn values of the late nineteenth century had been precisely their claim to be absolutes. The bourgeois world against which the Pirandellian spirits rebel had been too guilty of presumption, of an unjustified, complacent, even arrogant confidence in its social institutions, its customs and codes of behaviour, its scientific faith, for them to trust any belief bearing even the slightest implication of certainty.

Since the new form towards which the Pirandellian characters so passionately aspire – if it must differ from the one that has failed, if it must be, and not only seem, unassailable, absolute – cannot exist, is impossible in the real world, they do not like to explain or define it; they know theirs is an unappeasable need, an unattainable goal. They know, that is, that their loss is final; yet they resent it – they cannot resign themselves to the chaos of formlessness and of insignificance. This is their conflict, their drama. Exiled as they are in the limbo of formlessness, their drama is an existential condition not dissimilar from that of the souls of Dante's limbo, who 'without hope live in desire.' The Pirandellian characters mount the stage to bear witness to this existential condition, this conflict that is their drama. They declare their loss and their irrepressible need for what they have lost as well as their tragic knowledge that they cannot achieve what they seek and need: a universe of certainties, an absolute that would allow them to affirm themselves, values that would create and define a reality for them. They define their ultimate tragedy as that of being destined to pursue forever their lost unity in the chaos of endless disintegration, the drama of 'a life devoid of form yet longing for a form' (I 44).

The characters of many dramatists who came after Pirandello, more or less conscious of this destiny of the impossibility of attaining that unassailable, absolute reality, are resigned to the fall into formlessness and have made peace with chaos; they represent the definitive loss of an essential human dimension, and their theatre moves towards silence. But the Pirandellian characters, although they know that they will never arrive at an acceptable solution, do not cease to search for it, to declare their need for it, even to pursue utterly unsatisfactory solutions, so strong is their longing for form, for a reality that can be shared. They will assert, in *Right You Are, if You Think You Are*, their awareness of the relativity of reality and maintain an uneasy family ménage. They will choose, in *Henry IV*, a reality fixed by the history of eight hundred years earlier. In *Six Characters*, they will seek definitive artistic form, or, failing to obtain it from their creator, seek at least momentary expressive form in the acting of a theatrical company. The six characters are clearly driven by the need for a profound form of communication, impossible to obtain even through the eloquence of the highest artistic creation, let alone through a play whose plot exists only orally, in fragments, in a form that is still in flux, continually contested, wide open to betrayals of interpretation. They are conscious of pursuing only compromises, utterly unsatisfactory goals, because the satisfactory ones are unattainable or unknowable or non-existent; they even complain about the definitive artistic form that they seek with such persistence and intelligence as the best possible means of communication (and even as a guarantee of immortality), because artistic form, despite its eloquence, cannot avoid fixing and simplifying the reality it tries to represent, while real life is complex, rich, in endless flux.

This traumatic discovery of an irreparable loss is, then, the existential condition of Pirandello's characters and the cause of their insoluble conflict with life in our time; it is at the source of their author's inspiration. Pirandello's work is pervaded by compassion for the fate of contemporary humanity, the victim of that trauma and loss, and by a condemnation of false values, of the social myths of honour, respectability, manners, behind which the bourgeois world hid its moral void. His inspiration is essentially ethical in nature.

Just as the Pirandellian characters try to unmask those myths, so they argue with the artistic forms that had represented and celebrated them, especially bourgeois comedy – which had been dominating the Italian, indeed the European, stage for over half a century – the forms of which are assumed by some of these characters in order to decry their contradictions and their hollowness. Instead of opposing them uncompromisingly, these characters prefer to embody recognizable situations and people of a bourgeois reality in order to protest its alienating and alienated qualities; they present themselves to a public and even to professional actors familiar with the forms and content of bourgeois drama, wearing its clothing and using its language, in order to unmask its mechanical nature, its conventionality, its equivocal familiarity. They make passionate use of dialectics, as the bourgeois characters do to defend bourgeois conventions, but they do so in order to tear them apart, and to condemn reasoning itself as an abuse, a means of repressing free and genuine feelings, or at least to underline its function as a means of reaching a more acute awareness of the absurdity of one's suffering; they use words to complain about their inadequacy as a means of communication. They make use of all these means of communication to attest to their condemnation to incommunicability, and their need to communicate.

And while using the accepted, traditional theatrical forms to discredit them, the Pirandellian character also uses them to demonstrate the validity of new, experimental, open forms. The tragedy of the characters is irresolvable, and the new theatre must remain open, with no solutions. It must invade the outworn forms of bourgeois drama, break up its structure, invalidate its denouements, laugh at its conclusions, propose non-conclusions; it must tell the respectable audiences that that third act they are expecting is a fraud that should be suppressed, or ignored or dismissed with sardonic laughter, that even the physical space of the stage is a convention and can be profitably enlarged to include the orchestra, the lobby, the nearby streets, any imaginable place.

Pirandello reflects an important moment of the 'crisis of passage' from nineteenth-century positivist culture to the avant-garde culture of the twentieth century. But while many writers of his own and the following generation eagerly embraced a fashionable irrationalism and nihilism, Pirandello deplores and attempts to escape them. The rich discoveries of the irrational, of the subconscious, of multiplicity, could not compensate for the tragic loss of unity, which moved Pirandello to compassion and moral indignation.

The most important element of the positivist vision of reality had been the certainty, fostered by centuries of Aristotelianism and later by modern science, of the existence and knowability of an objective reality that included human beings but was not of their making; not a product of their ability to conceive, interpret, and incorporate inner concepts into their vision of exterior reality, as they had done through the centuries, from the earliest mythological interpretations of reality through the numberless philosophical systems from the pre-Socratics to Kant and Hegel, but an objective reality, which the human mind, especially after the introduction of the scientific method of inquiry some centuries earlier, had been exploring with increasing depth. The discoveries in the fields of the exact sciences were at the root of that certainty, but the overwhelming influence of Aristotelian thought through the centuries on the mental attitudes of people of average education accounted for the tendency to stretch that certainty beyond the limits of scientific knowledge to the social sciences, and even to individual and collective perceptions of inner and exterior realities. These are areas in which objective knowledge is impossible, and in which, therefore, no certainty, no dogmatism, was justifiable: areas in which consciousness can at most be subjective, a stream of opinions derived from a stream of totally subjective impressions and perceptions of a reality created by the individual to satisfy inner existential needs or by a dominant group able to impose its vision of things on others.

The relentless pressure of the group on the individual to conform usually succeeds. Because the conflict would be unendurable, the individual accepts, however reluctantly, the ideas, ideals, values, forms, and behaviours defined and proposed by society. But they constitute a mask, imposed and accepted under duress. Or the individual may refuse the mask, only to create another, personal one, in order to survive, to fight society with its own weapons, to function in it, or in spite of it, to communicate to others one's perception of oneself, to seek in others a confirmation of one's perception of oneself, of one's identity.

Thus, Mattia Pascal, who thought he could rid himself of a suffocating reality, must soon create for himself a new reality to face a society geographically different but equally exacting of the individual; and finally, oppressed by the later reality too, he escapes to return to the previous one – by which, however, since he is officially dead, he is relegated to a limbo that allows him no satisfactory social integration, though unwittingly allowing him a bit of the longed-for freedom. Thus, the Ponza family, having created the unusual family ménage that allows the two survivors of the real or fictitious loss of wife or daughter to go on living while they maintain their individual vision of reality, must fight, tooth and nail, a society that does not deem the creation of a private reality acceptable, let alone its externalization in social relationships. Thus, Henry IV, an object of derision for society even before the accident that caused his madness – a derision in which the joke that precipitated the accident was only one episode – creates for himself a new reality, when he awakens from twelve years of madness, in order to survive the new situation, and repay society to some degree for his loss; and after rejecting that new reality for a few hours, he might revive it at the end of the play, having killed the person most directly responsible for his loss.

But we are dealing always with imposed, subjective realities, all relative, not absolute, all different in content, fashioned by different individuals, even when a number of them think they have a very similar view of things, and therefore group together to try to impose it on the whole society. An objective reality, outside the field of the exact sciences, if it exists at all, is beyond our possibility of knowing it, and if we cannot know it, we cannot speak of it or even simply affirm its existence.

And if objective reality cannot be known, created reality becomes an inevitable necessity for everyone. 'I think that life is a very sad joke,' Pirandello wrote, 'because there is in us, we do not know how, or why or whence, the necessity of constantly deceiving ourselves with the spontaneous creation of a reality (one for each and never the same for all) which from time to time we discover to be vain and illusory.'[2] Even the madness Henry IV invents, in order to face the reality he wakes up to and take whatever little revenge he can on his persecutors, is accepted by the latter to confirm their opinion of their own sanity: they need not be too deeply shocked by his terrible words, if they are those of a madman. Hence even after the revelation of his recovery it will not be too difficult for them to become convinced once more of his madness and to consider Belcredi's murder the act of one mentally deranged, and not what it really is: a vindictive gesture made in blind rage by a man who has persuaded himself to re-enter the unforeseeable and uncontrollable present from an orderly and controlled reality fashioned after a known and totally predictable historical model.

This reality created by each individual with or against the pervasive or compelling pressure of other individuals or an entire group, being relative, illusory, personal, is not so different, in its fundamental subjectivity, from the created reality of a work of art. Art, however, conceived at a deeper level of consciousness, wrought upon by longer reflection, more acute intelligence, and more intense concentration, probably comes closer to achieving truth; it is, in Pirandello's words, 'less real, perhaps, but truer' (I 57). The reality created by the artist possesses qualities that the reality created by each individual in everyday life does not possess, and will lack some qualities characteristic of daily life: artistic reality is fixed forever in a definitive text, which, if genius has shaped it, may confer on the artistic creation and its characters an immortal vitality, while the reality created by everyday life is in flux, constantly changing, not capturable in memory, perishable. Artistic reality captures a particular moment, creates an ideal moment, frozen, abstracted from the context of the flux of everyday reality. In that respect it impoverishes the vitality that derives from movement, from multidimensionality, from contradiction, in favour of a vitality that comes from an ideal sublimation, a distillation of the most effective form of communication, artistic form.

The two realities, however, do have in common a basic subjectivity. And they maintain a strong interdependence: everyday reality to the eye of the 'humorist' (as Pirandello often called himself in his lengthy elaboration on the concept of literary 'humour' or *umorismo*) reveals the presence of a tragic contradiction; attempting to represent this, the humorist's art then expresses the feeling of the author before that tragic condition, 'the feeling for the opposite.' The work, in which the tragedy of the characters may be *less real, perhaps, but truer*, gives form to the artist's sense of the tragedy – *less true, perhaps, but more real* – of everyday reality. Art is not the mirror *of* life but a mirror *for* life. Life looking at itself would never be able to see the fundamental contradiction that is revealed to it when it looks at itself as it is mirrored in the work of art. Art holds up a mirror to life, which sees itself in it the way the artist's eye sees it, in its essence, its most secret reality – which is no less real. The 'humoristic' – that is, tragically contradictory – condition that art reveals is equally present, if unrevealed, in everyday reality. The 'humorist' laments that tragic reality in all sincerity, deeply, because it is real, is inherent in everyday life, and cannot merely be treated ironically as an exclusively 'fictitious' reality, belonging to the work of art alone.[3]

This is one of the reasons why Pirandello considered the term 'irony' inadequate to designate the attitude and approach that he chose to call *umorismo*. He rejected both irony as a term of traditional rhetoric, that is, saying something while meaning its opposite, a contradiction that is obvious, 'fictitious,' one of words not of substance;[4] and irony in the sense meant by Schlegel: 'for the poet irony consists in his never becoming totally one with his work, in his not losing, not even in moments of high emotions, the awareness of the unreality of what he creates, in not becoming the victim of the phantoms created by himself, in smiling at his reader who lets himself be caught up in the game, and even at himself who dedicates his own life to a game.'[5] The awareness of the 'humorist' goes beyond (it does not stop before taking that step, as some would have it)[6] the awareness of the unreality of the work of art, of the merely fantastic, fictitious elements that Schlegel reminds us of. The feeling of the 'humorist' springs from the awareness of the contradiction that tragically dominates everyday reality, all human life, before becoming the theme of the work of art. If the smile of the romantic poet, according to Schlegel, is born of the awareness that pathos is after all the soul of a fictitious work, the lament of the 'humorist' is born of the *feeling for* what in life, and not just in the work of art, is tragically reversed.

Pirandello's distinction between the comic and the humoristic lies in this tragic quality: 'the comic is the perception of the opposite'; it causes laughter because something is *amusingly* reversed; but if 'the perception of the opposite' is followed by reflection revealing the tragic underside of the comic and producing the *'feeling for* the opposite' – compassion for the victims of the contradiction – 'then I cannot laugh as before.' One is no longer confronting something amusingly overturned but something *tragically* overturned.[7] The humoristic is what at first prompts laughter but upon reflection must lead us to tears, to anguish.

The deep current of sympathy that ties the author to the 'Pirandellian' characters, the seriousness of the writer before their drama, is due not to the fact that he 'is not aware of the "unreality of what he creates,"'[8] but to the fact that his characters are the expression of a moral torment, 'the *feeling for* the opposite,' and embody in a *less real, perhaps, but truer* form the *less true, perhaps, but more real* tragedy of humanity in our time. It is a sympathy that is felt especially deeply when the 'Pirandellian' characters react with fierce indignation to any insult to their suffering, their sincerity, their authenticity – in a word to their human dignity.

Pirandello's whole concept of *umorismo* affirms, in fact, that his art springs from a matrix that is deeply ethical, not merely preoccupied with questions of form. And when he says that the characters in his work may be 'less real, perhaps, but truer,' he is talking about a truth not exclusively epistemological[9] but ethical as well, a truth concerned with good and evil, with injustice and understanding and compassion.

2 *Liolà*: Beyond Naturalism

Mita: Just words? I don't think so!
Aunt Croce: Yes, words, words! Because we're not deceitful, though we
seem to be! You are, though you don't seem to be!

(*Liolà*, II 739)

On first reading, *Liolà* might easily be perceived as a play in which naturalistic elements are strong, a play in which Pirandello returns to his
earlier stylistic sources. For a long time scholars have persisted in seeing it in this light.[1] Furthering this impression are the facts that it was
first written in Sicilian dialect, in the years in which Nino Martoglio
was continually urging Pirandello to write for a vernacular theatre that
he and his associates were trying to revitalize, and that the actor who
was to play Liolà was Angelo Musco, whose acting technique was
unquestionably naturalistic. Accordingly, both the drama and the character have been seen as having close affinities with Pirandello's much
earlier novels and short stories, earlier, that is, than *The Late Mattia Pascal* of 1903–4. *Liolà*, however, was written in 1916, and the presence of
some apparently naturalistic elements in a play of this date must at
least invite our questions.

According to one of the 'Letters Written to His Son Stefano during
World War One,'[2] it was, in fact, written in two short weeks during a
vacation in the summer of 1916. But the play must have been brooded
over for a long time, since it retrieves the name of one of the characters
of 'La mosca' (1904) and makes very skilful use of situations and plot
elements of *The Late Mattia Pascal*, as well as of the *commedia dell'arte*, of
Machiavelli's *Mandrake*,[3] and of classical comedy.[4] This long ancestry

too should prevent us from being deceived by the inclusion of some situations that are reminiscent of Verga's naturalism: such as the custom of farming out the harvesting of nut and grape crops to a poor relative, or of hiring day labourers in the village square, or of marrying a young woman to an old landowner (as in Verga, La Vespa is married to Uncle Crocifisso). When Tuzza makes love with Liolà to spite Mita, who, though now married, still enjoys the attentions of her old admirer, we may be reminded of Santuzza, who in *Cavalleria rusticana* makes love with Turiddu to spite Lola, or, in the story of the same title, reveals the Lola–Turiddu affair to Alfio. But all this is not exclusively Sicilian: the marriage between the young girl and the rich old man goes back to classical comedy, and the hiring of day labourers in the village square appears in the parables of the New Testament.

The fact is that the few things that Liolà and the other characters do because they are Sicilian are either not important to the thematic development of the play, or are used in a uniquely Pirandellian, 'humorist,' key. On the other hand, the things that Liolà does because he is Liolà would be no different if the action took place elsewhere; and they are what really counts in the development of the character and his function in the play.

Liolà is not the common peasant he might seem to a superficial spectator or to those who view him through the conventions of naturalism. He does not, for one thing, have the narrow, selfish mentality of the peasant of either Verga's or Pirandello's own naturalism (one remembers, for example, Gerlando's parents in Pirandello's 'The Black Shawl').[5] He is not a naturalistic character at all. He is a great invention of the author's imagination, vividly alive, 'humoristically' complex, and altogether functional in regard to the themes of the play. He embodies two human characteristics that are relevant to the themes, characteristics that may seem opposed but are actually complementary: the gaiety of a carefree man and the astuteness of a wise one.

Liolà is joyous, lively, lighthearted. Wherever he goes in his radiant joy, everyone grows happy, the girls go a little crazy ('he makes us all so happy ... and wherever he is, the girls are happy to go,' II 227), and they buzz around him like flies around honey. Only the old fogeys think of him as irresponsible ('crazy,' 'a breezy butterfly,' II 677, 743), dangerous (a 'goddam crook,' 'filthy,' a 'hoodlum,' 'spoiled meat,' II 667, 669, 673, 683), someone to stay away from. His *joie de vivre* makes him attractive to others, and he is content with himself as well. He is, in a word, quite free of the suffering characteristic of the 'Pirandellian' character (not one of his 'many ... far from happy characters').[6]

But Liolà's personality is not exclusively one of gaiety and lightheart-edness. Pirandello is not saying that the cheerful and carefree are con-tent with themselves[7] and thereby become successful in life, attractive, and likable. If Liolà were only gay and lighthearted he would not be so for long, but would soon be up to his neck in trouble; in fact, he would probably have already become the victim of some tragic settling of accounts, some fatal revenge.[8] The most important characteristic of Liolà is his awareness, and the astuteness that follows from it. He knows the way things are in this world; he knows the value of the hyp-ocritical conventions of society; and he acts accordingly – he exploits them. If on the one hand a carefree soul alone would cause him nothing but trouble, and on the other awareness alone would destroy his con-tentment, an awareness that engenders shrewdness makes him a happy man. The people around him suffer because they lack this existential adaptability ('we can't all be shrewd like you,' Mita tells Liolà, II 707). He uses his knowledge of 'the rules of the game' to avoid being oppressed by society, to beat society at its own game.

Thus, he goes through life singing, inspiring affection, making use of every possible circumstance to foster his success, even circumstances that might be damaging, like the existence of that nestful of illegitimate children, which, instead of serving as a constant warning (particularly to the girls who buzz around him), allows him to appear youthful and carefree on stage, playing and singing with them, more likable than ever, in a display of simplicity and paternal love.

Of course, whereas lightheartedness makes him attractive, his shrewdness makes him dangerous, and those girls who have been caught in his lure know it; like trapped game they prefer mutilation, leaving a child in his lap, but freeing themselves of him, rather than risking marriage ('all of them want me – and none of them want me!' II 705). Tuzza tells her mother: 'Listen, I don't want him! I don't! I don't!' (II 673); and even his mother, always eager to defend him when the gos-sip begins (e.g., 'You shouldn't say such things ... There's never been a more dutiful and loving son than my Liolà,' II 657), says decidedly: 'I wouldn't trust a man like Liolà with a dog of mine, let alone a daugh-ter!' (II 693). And in fact he is not one to submit willingly to the bonds of marriage, and he makes no bones about it; he says he is no 'tame bird' (II 679); though he makes the gesture of asking for Tuzza's hand, he is very glad when his offer is rejected (II 679).

However, the offer itself and the manner in which it is tendered, including his wish to be told by Tuzza herself before witnesses that she does not want him (II 681), are telling indications of his awareness and his cleverness; as is, indeed, his behaviour throughout the play, perhaps most strikingly in that extraordinary moment of intuitive penetration in the last scene of Act I, when Liolà sees Uncle Simone go into the house where Tuzza has taken refuge alone (II 677–9) and in an instant foresees all the possible consequences of that act and conceives his plan of action (II 679–81) in support of his childhood friend, Mita – a defence that will, however, include the enjoyment of a new and undoubtedly long-awaited sexual conquest.[9]

All his actions derive from his knowledge of the ways of the world. No less than Henry IV, Angelo Baldovino, Leone Gala, or many others, Liolà is the typical Pirandellian character in his consciousness of the absurdities of life, and of society's outrageous deceptions and hypocrisy, behind which it masks its moral bankruptcy. Liolà is different in that he does not become a victim but succeeds better than other Pirandellian characters in manipulating and mastering society. The others, even when they become manipulators, like Henry IV with his guests, or Baldovino, or Gala, do not escape a profound victimization themselves.

Liolà has constructed his own philosophy, according to which there are no moral or immoral actions in an absolute sense, only in a relative one. Not only is it foolish to want to be honest and noble, to act according to absolute moral principles, but to do so might even be dishonest and unjust. Somebody is going to stab you in the back, and you are guilty if, having the power to prevent it, you do not do so because you refuse to fight one unjust act with another (II 709 ff.). Yours would be an unjust act only by absolute, abstract standards inculcated by society, not in a relative sense, according to which, instead, it would be not only a just act, but a duty: 'God himself commands you to' (II 713). These are the arguments by which Liolà persuades Mita, who at the end of the second act swears that she will never commit one unjust act to prevent another ('Oh, no! Not that! Never!' II 711–13), while a little later, in the middle of the third act, she is pregnant, and comes on stage 'extremely calm' (II 737) to preach to those who had attempted to do her harm.

It is an egoistic, relativistic, even Machiavellian ethic, no doubt: circumstances and ends justify one's actions. It is quite different from the 'altruism' of which both Brose and Paolucci speak (cf. note 9), or from Cosmo Crifò's description of Liolà as 'a challenge to all pretence, as a victory over the hypocrisy and egoism that threaten spontaneity.'[10] Among the axioms of Liolà is the Machiavellian 'pretending is a virtue. If a man can't pretend, he can't rule' (II 665); as for spontaneity, Liolà's is rather like spontaneity in art: it is achieved only through profound awareness, consummate craftsmanship.

If it is his spontaneity and zest for life that attract his admirers in the first act of the play, in the third, when their initial reluctance and then their enthusiastic participation in the grape harvest with Liolà take on added meaning, it becomes evident that it is not only Liolà's gaiety that attracts them; they are equally, perhaps more powerfully, drawn by his cleverness. They are all overjoyed at the news of the new turn of events in Mita's life, to some degree perhaps because they feel that a wrong has been righted, but especially because it was righted through the cleverness of their hero Liolà. It is the celebration of triumphant shrewdness familiar in so many Boccaccio stories, of the victory of the underdog in popular fiction (rather than, say, of the success of the learned and rich young protagonist of Machiavelli's *The Mandrake*).

The play illustrates and dramatizes the hypocrisy and contradictions that plague the modes of behaviour to which society attaches so much importance; it is especially concerned with the value of appearances and the relativity of every moral principle in a society that, instead, constantly attempts to impose absolute moral principles. These themes at first alternate, later become intertwined in the play, and finally develop in unity as the character of Liolà emerges and his dramatic function becomes clear. One of the roots of Liolà's shrewdness, in fact, is his awareness of the value that this society, which preaches absolute standards and principles, in actual fact assigns to appearances, and of what this society is prepared to do to save them.

A girl burdened with an illegitimate pregnancy is dishonoured, but if a marriage proposal is made and accepted, no matter how unsavoury the match, her honour is saved. In this case, however, Tuzza and her mother choose dishonour, not because of their allegiance to a more rational and less hypocritical moral code, but because the possibility of a more lucrative bargain exists: Tuzza prefers to live with her dishonour so that her child will pass as the child of Zio Simone and thus become heir to his fortune. Zio Simone accepts the bargain because the dishonour of his sterility is also redeemed in this hypocritical society by the fathering of children, legitimate or otherwise. In fact, his wife too will erase the dishonour of her sterility with an illegitimate pregnancy obtained with the cooperation of Liolà, and the dishonour of its illegitimacy by denying the latter with the cooperation of her husband.

These are the absurdities perpetrated by a hypocritical society. The honour of the unmarried girl threatened by a pregnancy is saved by marriage, any marriage, however corrupt; the honour of the married threatened by sterility is saved by any pregnancy – however scandalous. These situations are the results of others, equally absurd, that have preceded them: the old landowner *must* marry in order to father an heir and avoid the 'tragedy' of leaving his patrimony to strangers or to distant relatives (II 651, 709, etc.); and to increase the probability of having children he *must* marry a young, 'beautiful, blooming' woman, who is 'bursting with health' (II 655), even if by doing so the probability of future discontent, jealousy, discord, rebellion, and infidelity increases. All his relatives, all the townspeople, urge him to do so – so things must be in this society. And her whole family, and the whole town, urge the young woman to marry him ('Was it my fault if, being a minor, they married me to somebody else? ... It wasn't my fault ... Only God knows whom I really loved when I got married,' II 701, 709), as if it were unparalleled good fortune to give birth to a child who will inherit all that wealth, even if she will have to put up with an old goat, stingy, jealous, irascible, sexually exhausted – but rich.

All this occurs in a society that claims to be based on, and to conduct itself according to, absolute moral principles (marriage is an institution that crowns reciprocal love; pregnancy is legitimate only in marriage; absolute fidelity to a sterile husband who mistreats his wife because of her alleged sterility is required; an injustice cannot be justified because it is aimed at preventing another injustice; evil must not be returned for evil; a wrong cannot be righted by another wrong). It tries to impose these on its members ('That would be a mortal sin!' II 655), while in fact practising a relativistic morality (marriage is sought not for absolute ideals, but to legitimize a pregnancy – in most cases compounding one mistake with another – or to facilitate the process of transmitting property; children are sought for the same utilitarian purpose; etc.). This hypocrisy is condemned in the play as a means to oppress the defenceless members of society. Tuzza is able, up to a point, to defend herself against this hypocrisy, exploiting it and trying to beat society at its own game, with the methods used by Liolà. Mita is the defenceless creature who is victimized by it as long as she remains faithful to the absolute morality society has drilled into her, until she too decides to adopt Liolà's philosophy of relativistic morality.

This is the hypocrisy of 'The License,' in a society that professes faith in science but in actuality believes in the evil eye. It is the hypocrisy of 'The Truth' and 'The Jinglebell Hat,' where society predicates his wife's infidelity as the deepest dishonour for the husband, a dishonour that can be wiped out only by a 'crime of honour,' that is, by the killing of the lovers, and then condemns the husband to jail for homicide. Liolà reveals the hypocrisy in the transactions of capitalism as well, based on laws that again claim to be absolute, while in fact 'the law might be changed tomorrow':

> Here you have a piece of land. You stand there looking at it, what does it produce? Nothing ... Well, I come to this piece of land of yours, I hoe it, I fertilize it, I dig a hole, I throw a seed into it: a tree comes up. Who's the earth given that tree to? To me! You come along and say no, that it's yours. Why yours? Because the land is yours? But does the land know, Zio Simone, who it belongs to? It gives the fruits to whoever works it. You take them because you clamp your foot on it, and because the law is on your side. But the law might be changed tomorrow! (II 669)

Liolà rejects this hypocrisy, this claim to, and imposition of, an absolute morality in an existential context marked everywhere by practices that are clearly relativistic. They must be condemned; their absurdity, their injustice, the oppression they exercise over the most innocent victims for the advantage of the most guilty must be demonstrated. Let absolutes be abandoned and there will be no more innocent and guilty, oppressor and oppressed.

This is the negative, destructive thrust of Liolà's philosophy. Pirandello, however, in this original and multidimensional character, suggests a new, positive code of behaviour. Since unfortunately society does not change easily and the exploitation perpetrated in the name of absolute social morality is difficult to eradicate, Liolà's proposal is a call to consistency, at least – consistency as the only possible redemption from the hypocrisy of absolutist morality.

This is precisely the desire of Chiarchiaro in 'The License,' who demands that his notoriety as a carrier of the evil eye be given official recognition, so that the advantages would balance the disadvantages in a society that professes supreme faith in the absolute truths of science, but actually believes in the evil eye; or of the protagonists of 'The Truth' and 'The Jinglebell Hat': that a society which condemns a husband dishonoured by the infidelity of his wife, and insists that such a dishonour must be erased by the killing of the lovers, must either stop jailing those who redeem themselves by a 'crime of honour,' or maintain absolute secrecy concerning the affair between the lovers; or of Baldovino in *The Pleasure of Honesty*,[11] who undertakes to protect the honour of the Marquis Colli and Miss Agata Renni by marrying her, but expects from them the honourable behaviour they would like only to simulate.

Thus, Liolà proposes and pursues a consistent vision and behaviour that renders just, in a relative sense, even a situation that might be considered unjust or false if taken in absolute terms. The moral dimension of social behaviour is relative, not absolute, and can be made authentic only if social behaviour is consistent with the moral relativism that actually prevails. This redemption may therefore start at any moment in life, no matter how low one has fallen. There is no need for dramatic conversions, great changes in one's behaviour, but only a change of attitude towards one's own pretence; authenticity comes with the elimination of hypocrisy, transforming pretence into sincerity. Society puts great value on appearances; then it must stop preaching absolute moral principles. Let it value appearances, but let it first admit that it does so – let it stop trying to conceal reality with a moral smoke screen that is continually torn by everyday practice. Consistency is a fundamental characteristic of nature; society should adopt it, and the morality of its behaviour would be authentic, even if its starting points were not so.

Among the supposedly honourable characters of the society represented in this play, the despised Liolà is the only one whose behaviour is honourable, because he knows what kind of person he is, admits it openly, accepts the consequences of his behaviour (the children, even marriage if necessary), and does not at all hide the fact that he exploits the hypocrisy of those who value appearances but do not want to admit it.

Liolà, contrary to what some critics have said (cf., for example, Crifò, p. 34, who sees *Liolà* 'as a challenge to all pretence'), does not want dissimulation totally eliminated from social behaviour; it is hypocrisy, falseness, that must be eliminated. Dissimulation must be practised like a Machiavellian 'virtue,' when it is necessary in order to achieve a just, 'relatively' moral end, and is not hypocritical mystification; it must be recognized as such, admitted, and employed consistently, honestly, so to speak; then it may even become respectable, redeem itself. An authentic life may be the result. An enormous injustice may be righted (the situation of Mita and Chiarchiaro) by consistency within pretence; an entire life can be honestly rebuilt, redeemed (as in *The Pleasure of Honesty*) by consistency, even in a situation of admitted dissimulation.

Dissimulation is the mask that everybody is more or less compelled to wear, from Liolà to Henry IV. Those who are aware of, and admit, it, unlike their bourgeois opponents who profess absolute truth and honesty, succeed in using it to their advantage, or even to laudable ends, beating society at its own game – certainly with eminently positive results: if the hypocritical regard for appearances may lead to the commission of an injustice (against Mita), then a conscious, consistent respecting of appearances (by Liolà, Mita, and even Zio Simone) can and does in *Liolà* re-establish justice, albeit a 'relative' one. Similarly, in *The Pleasure of Honesty* the two young lovers have embarked on an adventure that according to the absolute moral precepts of society is illegitimate; they should accept its consequences, the birth of an illegitimate child. If instead they refuse to accept the consequences of their illegitimate behaviour, if they seek a remedy in the false legitimacy of a marriage of convenience, they must at least accept the consequences of the remedy, and make it a genuine, honest pretence, as Baldovino wishes it to be, not the transparent screen the two 'honourable' characters desire. The struggle to emerge from the shipwreck of one's life through a consistent assumption of the responsibilities imposed by the pretence inherent in the remedy is a high enough price to pay for the redemption that is sought.

This redemption does not take place only on the abstract level of conscience, nor through an abstract dialectical process, but at the level of moral conduct, in the authenticity that all suffering generates. Thus, in *Right You Are, if You Think You Are* neither Mr Ponza nor Mrs Frola want to lie for the sake of lying. Their 'subjective' truth is redeemed because it is lived and suffered through with such dramatic torment.

Liolà is, then, a play *characteristically inspired by the feeling for the real suffering* born of the fundamental opposition of the recalcitrant Pirandellian character and the society by which he feels oppressed. This is also the most 'humoristic' aspect of this supposedly 'joyful' play, 'full of songs and sun' (cf. 'Letters to Stefano'). On close observation one realizes that there is a great deal of suffering around Liolà, beginning with the girls that fly around him like butterflies, or wasps, as they are variously called at different moments of the play, who live in a torment of continuous attraction and repulsion: they must follow him and keep their distance at the same time. But those who suffer most deeply are the three characters who interact with Liolà: Tuzza, Mita, and even Simone, whose role is certainly that of antagonist in this play. He is not a comic character, as is Nicia in *The Mandrake*, for instance, who (contradicting his honourable position in society and the pretence to wisdom implied in his law degree) plays the part of the dupe who practically cuckolds himself, so to speak. Simone might superficially be considered a comic figure somewhat similar to Nicia, but on closer reading he must be seen as a 'humoristic' figure: he wants not only a son, but redemption from the stigma of sterility; he wants public recognition of his legitimate fatherhood; and he finds it and imposes it through the process of suffering typical of the most 'humoristic' Pirandellian figures, a process that includes the more or less conscious adoption of the despised relativistic logic and ethics of his antagonist, Liolà.

Thus, their relationship too is quite different from that of the antagonists/allies of *The Mandrake*, in which the victory of the shrewd protagonist Callimaco corresponds more or less to the defeat of old Nicia; the latter, just when he should oppose Callimaco, comically becomes his ally, because, hardly the wise and learned man he claims to be, he turns out to be a credulous fool. In *Liolà* the two antagonists behave like antagonists, yet both emerge more or less victorious from their enterprise – a rather unusual outcome and far more complex than the denouement of traditional comedy.

Those who draw easy parallels between *Liolà* and *The Mandrake* might also do well to compare the typical structure of traditional comedy, including a classical play like *The Mandrake*, with that of *Liolà*. In traditional comedy, the protagonist, seeking the realization of his goals, meets with obstacles, undergoes temporary setbacks caused by the opposing forces (an individual antagonist, or the opposition of society as such, etc. – protagonist and antagonist may even personify the opposing forces of good and evil), until at a climactic point, in a crucial trial (at the end of the second or the beginning of the third act in a three-act structure), which is successfully overcome by the protagonist, a satisfactory ending is achieved, a 'happy ending,' and the total dissolution of all difficulties. The plot of *Liolà* is unquestionably more complex, a structure quite different from the traditional one.

In the *first act* the protagonist Liolà comes, reluctantly, to ask for Tuzza's hand; he is rejected, and he is very happy; it is a victory for him. Tuzza, afflicted with a pregnancy she does not want, instead of recognizing Liolà as the father, bargains with Simone, a transaction that is advantageous to both; like Liolà, she too is victorious. Her victory damages Simone's wife Mita, who is the victim so far, and whose setbacks begin in the first act and continue until the last scene of the *second act*. Mita, that is, who is not herself the protagonist, is undergoing the setbacks that in traditional comedy usually befall the protagonist. The latter is supposed to struggle, no matter what the obstacles and setbacks, until the crucial trial and triumph. Instead, Mita lets herself be reproached, cursed, beaten by her husband; she leaves him and his house practically in the hands of her rival; she is sought out by the husband, who orders her home while insisting that he will bring home Tuzza's child when it is born; she refuses to cuckold him; that is, she renounces the struggle, which is instead carried on by the one who should properly do so, the protagonist Liolà, until the final victory – a victory that belongs to them both. In the *third act*, in fact, that victory is externalized. It is both a material and, more importantly, a philosophical victory for Liolà, and an eminently social victory for Mita (and consequently, and for different reasons, for Simone). But the celebration of these victories must remain deeply ambiguous. Liolà openly celebrates, with his songs, and the procession of girls celebrates with him, a victory that cannot openly be spoken of. Mita and Simone openly declare their victory but cannot join in the celebration led by Liolà, because their victory, although of course connected with his, cannot openly be connected with his – which, as far as public opinion is concerned, must remain unacknowledged.

It is, then, a new structure that confronts us, considerably more complex than that of traditional comedy: the protagonist struggles as the traditional protagonist does, but instead of undergoing obstacles and setbacks until the crucial test from which he emerges victorious, here he is victorious at the end of the first act, at the end of the second, at the end of the third, indeed throughout the entire third act. His antagonist, Simone, also seems able to twist circumstances to his advantage at every occasion; thus, he is a party to Tuzza's victory at the end of the first act and to Mita's at the end of the third.[12]

Those who undergo the vicissitudes usually reserved for the protagonist (or the forces of good), who encounters nothing but difficulties and setbacks at first, only to triumph in the end, and for the antagonist (or the opposing forces), who at first seems to be triumphant but then must yield to the protagonist, are the deuteragonists, Mita and Tuzza. The latter personifies the opposing forces, apparently victorious in the first and second acts only to be defeated in the end; Mita, who seems destined for defeat in the first and second acts, is victorious in the end.

The play is, then, *closely structured on Pirandello's 'relativistic' vision* – a vision confirmed, of course, by the dramatic action: the success of Liolà's enterprises and the conversion of his adversaries to his view of life. It is not, however, that dialectics are absent, especially in the verbal clashes between Liolà and Simone, and Liolà and Mita; Liolà's considerable ability as a logician is expressed in these verbal contests (a frequent activity of the most representative Pirandellian characters), although the action of the play never lets up.

To complement its complex structure and to keep its tension alive, a protagonist at least as substantial and consequential as a Henry IV, a Baldovino, or the Father of the *Six Characters* is needed; and in fact, as soon as Liolà makes his entrance, the folkloric backdrop of the nut harvest fades, everything begins to revolve around him, and he moves front and centre as a challenge to the opposing forces. In a parallel to the structure of the first act, Liolà enters in the middle of the second as well, but the action presupposes his presence from the very beginning: his children and Gesa, the girls running after the children and Gesa because they assume *he* is there, their talk alluding to him. And after Liolà enters, whether he engages in small talk or in a serious discussion, whether he hides behind the door or circumvents Simone or sneaks into Gesa's house, he directs the action of the play. The third act practically cannot start without him and begins in earnest only when he arrives with his followers. After a brief absence during which Simone and Mita have delivered a mortal blow to Tuzza's aspirations, Liolà returns to wrap things up, demonstrating to all those who would like to stick him with Tuzza now, especially Zio Simone, the moral of the play: they should at least be consistent in their pretences; if it were to be claimed now that Tuzza's child is not Simone's, no one would believe that Mita's child is his either.

This play, then, is *built around a character who is hardly naturalistic, but is instead a highly imaginative creation, and a perfectly functional one*. The *raisonneur* of the grottesco theatre, always a secondary character, representing in part the dramatist's own ideas and his manipulation of characters and situations (as is Laudisi in *Right You Are, if You Think You Are*), here becomes the main character, asserting a vision and more importantly translating his view of life into dramatic action through his own sheer ability and his magnificent manipulation of situations, characters, human destinies.

Hence the naturalistic forms vanish at the end of the very first scene, which flows into an action functional to the central themes of the play: the dialectical opposition between what seems and what is, the contradictions in social behaviour and the oppression of the individual that those contradictions cause when absolute principles are imposed or when people try erroneously to hang on to them.

In fact, *not even the language of this play is naturalistic*, beginning with the Italian itself, which, apart from the six verses of the 'Passion' and the very few proverbs (which seem numerous only because they appear in twos and threes), is much closer to Tuscan than to Sicilian. In fact, the Tuscan idioms are more numerous than the Sicilian ones, and a comparison between the dialect and the Italian version of the play reveals a strong effort to minimize regional expressions and to produce an at least equally idiomatic text in the national tongue.[13]

3 *Right You Are, if You Think You Are*: The Reality of Appearances

---

> They themselves have obliterated those factual data ... and they've created a fantasy that has all the solidity of reality ... and now you're condemned to the exquisite torture of having before you both the illusion and the reality, and being unable to distinguish one from the other!
>
> (*Right You Are, if You Think You Are*, I 1041)

In *Liolà* the problem of the opposition between appearances and reality inspired the creation of a vividly imagined character, whose personality 'humoristically' dramatizes the reconciliation of two apparently opposing elements, a lighthearted gaiety and a wise shrewdness. Presumably mutually exclusive, they are in fact, as we have seen, complementary and interdependent. This opposition, which is resolved within the character in a functional moral relativism, also manifests itself outwardly in Liolà's clash with a world professing social norms based on moral absolutes but too often in conflict with them in daily practice, a conflict that causes social discord and a great deal of social unhappiness.

In *Right You Are, if You Think You Are* the opposition between appearances and reality is dramatized chiefly in the conflict that arises between a group of three Pirandellian characters and the familiar group of conventional, self-righteous bourgeois characters; when the first group act upon their relativistic view of reality, they profoundly disturb the latter, whose prying and intolerance unleash a virtual 'inquisition' (I 1070) upon the nonconformists.

Pirandello distinguishes the two groups clearly through his characteristically specific stage directions as well as his dramatic dialogue, which reflect their profound inner differences. The bourgeois inquisitors are presented in the typical middle-class parlour setting of the bourgeois theatre. Amalia is a woman 'in her mid-forties; her ostentatiously self-important manner is due to the position her husband occupies in society. She gives you to understand, however, that, were it completely up to her, she would act her part, and behave quite differently, on many occasions' (I 1011). Dina, 'nineteen, has the air of one who thinks she understands everything better than Mom, and even Dad' (ibid.). Mrs Sirelli, 'plump, red-cheeked, still young,' is 'decked out with overdone provincial elegance; burning with restless curiosity; sharp with her husband' (I 1014); the latter, 'bald, forty-ish, fat,' has 'greased hair, pretensions to elegance, shiny, squeaky shoes' (ibid.). Mrs Cini is 'a silly old woman, full of avid malice poorly concealed by an affectation of naivety' (ibid.); Mrs Nenni, 'an even sillier and more affected old lady,' is 'just as avidly curious, but more wary, frightened' (I 1045). Agazzi, 'fifty years old, unkempt, red hair, bearded, gold-rimmed spectacles,' is described as 'authoritarian, irritable' (I 1020). The prefect, 'sixty-ish, tall, fat,' has 'an air of superficial affability' (I 1066). Complacent masters of a world in which everything is as it should be, they cut everybody down to their own size; convinced of the existence of absolute truth, they pursue it relentlessly.

The inquisitors' victims have arrived at a truth of their own through years of suffering and patient adjustment ('it's a real tragedy ... which through terrible privation and suffering we have been able to deal with' I 1033), and now are determined to defend their hard-won conquest tooth and nail. As in the case of their persecutors, the stage directions that describe them forcefully project their inner nature: Mrs Frola, 'a neat little old lady, modest, very pleasant,' has 'eyes full of an enormous sadness tempered by her constant sweet smile' (I 1021); Mr Ponza, 'stocky, dark skinned, almost savage-looking, dresses entirely in black, thick, black hair, low forehead, thick, black moustache, clenches his fists constantly, speaks with an effort, in fact with barely contained violence; at intervals dries his brow with a black-bordered handkerchief. When he talks, his eyes remain hard, fixed, and grim' (I 1027); Mrs Ponza, 'stiff, in mourning dress, her face hidden by a thick black veil' (I 1076), speaks 'solemnly and sombrely' (I 1077).

Laudisi is a different character altogether, connected with neither of these two groups of antagonists; he is the detached chorus, the *raisonneur* of the grottesco theatre, representative and expositor of the ideas of the author. His is a multiple dramatic function absent from the bourgeois theatre and infrequent in Pirandello's work, part author, part director, part puppet master; he reflects, in intellectual terms, the contrast played out in the dramatic action between the Pirandellian and the bourgeois characters.

This relationship between the theoretical level and the level of the dramatic action foreshadows the relationship between the world of reality and that of art which will be explored fully in *Six Characters* and *Each in His Own Way*: thanks to the detachment that creative activity imposes, the artist can penetrate and understand reality more deeply than those who live immersed in it.

To the inquisitors the possibility of objective, absolute truth is not problematic; they have never questioned the assumption that it exists and is attainable. Laudisi agrees that some truths can be known ('*Mrs Cini*: But then, oh Lord, we know nothing with certainty! *Laudisi*: What do you mean, nothing! Why nothing? Let's not exaggerate! Pardon me, the days of the week, how many are there? *Mrs Cini*: Well, seven. *Laudisi*: Monday, Tuesday, Wednesday ... *Mrs Cini*: ... Thursday, Friday, Saturday ... *Laudisi*: ... and Sunday! And the months of the year? *Mrs Cini*: Twelve! *Laudisi*: January, February, March ...' I 1047), truths involving mathematical and scientific facts; but he seeks to convince them that in the realm of human emotions, of personal opinions and beliefs, of the value of moral principles and behaviour, truth can never be absolute: it is subjective, personal, mutable, relative, and may be known only in those terms. It is absurd to assume the existence of absolute truths in these spheres and worse to expect that they can be known. If his niece were to place the cook's slippers on his desk, it would be relatively easy to establish the identity of the objects and their ownership, but such knowledge would be of very little use or interest. The *reason* for her act would be the focus of interest, and certainly not easily determinable. It is a known fact that Mrs Frola cannot enter her daughter's home, and that Mr Ponza allows her to communicate with her daughter only from a distance. But the reason behind these facts is totally different in the minds of the two Pirandellian characters, sincere as both are. However, Laudisi's relatives and their guests cannot admit that both may be right.

The dramatic action in fact consists of an obstinate search for one absolute, objective truth. Pirandello called this play a 'parable' because it dramatizes so clearly the themes of the subjectivity of truth, and of the difficulty of communicating one's own truth to others. All the elements of the work are designed to achieve this end.

1. The action that takes place in the typical middle-class parlour is made to seem perfectly recognizable, as are the characters with their bourgeois mentality and prying gossip, with their acritical assumption

that an objective truth both exists and can be established, an assumption characteristic of the bourgeoisie of the Victorian age of positivism.
It is in this period that Pirandello sets his play, and its ambiance is that
of the traditional bourgeois theatre, which virtually dominated the Italian stage in that era. But Pirandello immediately introduces into this
world contrasting forces that precipitate the dramatic action. They
represent important counter-currents in late Victorian society, in which
the dominant positivistic mentality was already deeply shaken by
spiritualism and irrationalism of all sorts: decadence, modernism, neo-
idealism, etc. etc.

The behaviour impelled by the bourgeois mentality is not simply
presented in the documentary manner characteristic of positivistic realism. Pirandello cleverly heightens the tension in the characters in
search of an objective truth by presenting them with a dilemma so absolutely simple as to appear absolutely resolvable: whether Mrs Ponza is
or is not the daughter of Mrs Frola – a device not unlike those employed
in detective fiction, intended to stimulate the investigative zeal of the
characters as well as the interest of the audience. Hence the development of the action differs from that of a traditional play with a happy
ending, and is more akin to that of a detective story, except for the
Pirandellian 'surprise' ending, a resolution entirely dictated by the
action of the drama, but unexpected and unsatisfactory for the investigators in this case, or in general for the audience accustomed to the predictable endings of the bourgeois theatre.

The bourgeois investigators, and the audience, are led step by step to
their perception of the simple nature of the dilemma by a process that
must inevitably stimulate and justify the mounting curiosity, indignation, and determination of people who are so insistent on social conventions (cf. their discussion about the propriety and norms of their
first visit to Mrs Frola, I 1001–19), and on the deference due them on the
basis of their social position, who bank on the normalcy and conformity
of the society they live in, as guarantors of the security and stability of
their well-being. Inquisitors, and audience, perceive first the strangeness of the Ponzas' ménage; then the defences Mr Ponza is trying to
preserve around that ménage; then, after the first breach has occurred,
the contradictions in the explanations of their family arrangements furnished by Mr Ponza and Mrs Frola; finally the reluctant but clear reciprocal accusations of various degrees of mental derangement. The 'facts'
emerge not as in a cold and merely verbal police interrogation; they are
painfully lived out under the very eyes of the seekers of the truth.

2. The technique of heightening suspense is accompanied by the

maintenance of a reasonable degree of verisimilitude in the presentation of the dramatic events, which are always within the realm of the possible. This is true from the very first scenes, where the initial background information is conveyed in a vivid but traditional manner. It is information that reveals a rather strange situation, excites curiosity, but is nevertheless believable; and the first attempt by Mrs Frola to explain the otherwise inexcusable behaviour of her son-in-law is acceptable as sufficiently plausible, at least until Mr Ponza contradicts her with an equally plausible but different explanation. The situation thus charged with questions then allows Laudisi to play on it with the Agazzis and their guests, agreeing and disagreeing with their opinion as to who is mentally deranged. The same occurs after each subsequent 'clarification': each of the two in turn presents such a plausible version of the facts as to put in doubt the version just furnished by the other; each explanation is so well thought out and put forward as to favour the presumption of its author's sanity.

Each clarification elicits further curiosity and calls for further explanations until the final apparition, simply because the two versions continue to be contradictory and include the reciprocal accusation of madness. Mr Ponza accuses Mrs Frola almost from the very beginning. The latter, solicitous and reticent, claims that she is seeking to excuse, not to accuse, her son-in-law ('Oh, God, you people are trying to reassure me, while I, on the contrary, want to reassure you about him!' I 1032), and never talks of madness, but even her virtuoso circumlocutions cannot avoid suggesting that he is mad. Pirandello brilliantly dramatizes their attachment to the reality they have created for themselves, and which they feel the need to defend even if it means hurting each other, despite their awareness that they need each other in their common struggle against the inquisitorial group.

The verisimilitude of the development of the action and its background and the adoption of several theatrical conventions of the bourgeois theatre are an important part of Pirandello's subversive dramatic strategy. They are designed to make the bourgeois characters (and the audience?) feel at ease, at home in their own environment, facing a comprehensible situation, believing that they can get to the bottom of it, convinced that their inquiry is perfectly reasonable and justifiable. In fact, those very elements of verisimilitude, the posing of a problem apparently so simple in a context apparently so close to 'normal,' impel the bourgeois characters towards a need for definitive explanation. But the 'conclusive' explanation, when it finally comes, will vindicate the position of the Pirandellian characters, not least because the two separate truths they persist in maintaining throughout the play have been presented with such plausibility that they demand acceptance. That is, the carefully crafted aura of similitude in the dramatic action forces on us the reality of truths that do not coincide. This adherence to verisimilitude is also reflected in the language of the play, which is consistently naturalistic, even in moments of high tension, or in the oracular utterances of Mrs Ponza.

3. It is clear that under the sustained realism of the surface the disturbing critical consciousness of the 'humorist' writer is at work, the awareness of the artist, expressed particularly through the character of Laudisi, who pauses to contemplate the spectacle of life and to perceive the futility of much human behaviour, and indirectly to invite the audience to share his perception. Meanwhile, Pirandello ironically reminds us, those who are totally immersed in everyday reality obstinately pursue their search without ever coming to a realization of its futility, or of the suffering it causes.

From an initial position of detachment, Laudisi formulates the ultimate truth, emphasizing it with his laughter after each block of action, which is designed to dramatize the truth but which fails to pierce the closed minds of his relatives. He is therefore compelled to become increasingly involved in the action, to the point where he takes it into his own hands. Earlier in the play he tries to avoid getting that involved. When, for instance, he appeals to his relatives to give up their inquiry, he might have been heard with less indifference had he appealed to their pity, stressing the suffering of their victims; instead, he appeals only to their intelligence, pointing out the inevitable futility of their search. Having failed to convince them, he is compelled to take things into his own hands and suggest that they move on to the logical solution of interviewing the recluse, thus forcing the play to a logical conclusion in the dramatization of the philosophical truth he has so often and futilely repeated for three acts.

The two groups have different inner needs, and perceive and respond to them differently. The bourgeois are predisposed to extroversion, confession, the communication of a reality perceived as plausible, accessible, objective, universal. Their victims are guarded, reserved; they perceive their neighbours' help as invasive, 'an outrageous harassment' (I 1070). From this 'relentless inquisition' (ibid.) they must defend the private, individual truth, which for them is not merely a theory, an intellectual attainment as it is for Laudisi, but a conquest that cost years of suffering, of patient adjustment: for Ponza it is 'a work of charity that cost me great suffering and sacrifice' (ibid.); for his wife it is a 'remedy that our compassion has shown us' (I 1077); 'it's a real tragedy,' Mrs Frola says, 'which through terrible privation and suffering we've been able to deal with by agreeing to live the way we live' (I 1033).

They are not individuals who reject 'the principle of sociability' (as Orazio Costa, who has often directed this play, would have us believe);[1] they reject only a 'sociability' that threatens to deny and destroy the reality, the individual truth, they have so painstakingly, painfully built. The need of the Pirandellian characters to feel vitally connected to their social environment is no less strong than that of their bourgeois coun-terparts; in fact, it is more intense because the communication of their individual identity has become problematic, nearly impossible. They too are engaged in an intense search for the self, for identity, for their own truth. And though they know they will never reach an objective, absolute truth, they need support and confirmation of the subjective, temporary truth they do achieve, to break their isolation, to overcome the anguish of their solitude; they seek this confirmation in the accep-tance of their own truth by others. The consensus of others helps them keep their own truth alive ('he needs to convince other people, he can't help it! To feel sure himself, you understand?' I 1035). For the Pirandel-lian characters it is just as difficult to communicate one's truth in a way that will compel that consensus, as it is to find the truth itself.

In reality this is everyone's drama. But those who believe in one absolute, objective, communicable truth are not aware that it is theirs as well; in contrast, the Pirandellian characters are intensely aware that it is their fundamental drama, and no matter how convinced they are of the difficulty and even the impossibility of human communication, they do not abandon their effort to achieve it – it is for them a funda-mental human need they cannot renounce.

Mr Ponza and Mrs Frola cannot, therefore, reject 'the principle of sociability' in their dialogue with their self-righteous neighbours. They are only reluctant to furnish the weapons that might be used to destroy what they have created through much suffering, but in fact they are extremely eager to communicate their own perception of their identity, their own truth, and to seek recognition.

Their problem lies in the fact that their truths do not coincide. This duality of truth is the root of the dissatisfaction and anxiety of those who seek *one* truth (as well as of the audience, who may sympathize with the victims, but in fact subconsciously shares the desire of the clearly obnoxious inquisitors for an absolute, objective truth). The very intensity and sincerity with which the two relate the history of their present situation – which, if anything, should indicate their firm belief in the reality they are revealing, and should further communication and understanding – are interpreted as obfuscations of the truth. And their honest efforts to explain their situation as logically as possible are perceived as efforts to confuse it. At a certain point the inquisitors begin to feel they themselves are being driven to the brink of madness.

Yet their victims had only tried to tell the truth, their own truths. Tragically, they remain incomprehensible to the inquisitors who refuse to accept a truth they have forged for themselves, even to grant them the right to forge it, and thus miss the chance to understand the reasons for what is perceived as a cover-up for 'God knows what mystery!' (I 1026). But if the two victims have failed to communicate their truths, they succeed in protecting them even when they are brought face to face, and even when, after the failure of the inquiry by their hometown police, the radical solution of questioning the recluse herself is proposed.

Not only in her appearance in the final moments, but throughout the play, Mrs Ponza is presented as the projection of the two distinct truths of Mr Ponza and Mrs Frola, and thus in her final statement she has no hidden individual identity that she wants to conceal; she furthers and brings to its necessary conclusion her sole function in the play: she is, and speaks as, the person one believes her to be. Finally given the opportunity to define herself definitively, she defines herself as the others had defined her. She plots in their favour, so to speak. She stops the progress of the inquiry. She compels the audience to accept the reality of subjective truth, which is of course what Laudisi has tried to do time and time again in the play.

But she achieves no greater success than he with the inquisitors, for whom she clarifies nothing. They are more unsettled than ever, but they do not understand; truth remains as veiled to them as her face. Between the two groups there exists an insurmountable obstacle that the three Pirandellian characters have tried to overcome in the effort to communicate *their* sense of reality, while the inquisitors have experienced only an increasing sense of frustration, and are left in the end 'stunned and disappointed' (I 1077).

4 *Six Characters*: The Tragic Difficulty of Human Communication

> The delusion of mutual understanding ... is the passion and torment ... of each one of them.
>
> ('Preface' to *Six Characters*, I 38)

Approaching *Six Characters* by way of Pirandello's earlier masterpieces makes its major themes easier to understand. There is, we even recognize, more than one Laudisi eager to help us interpret them. But it is clear from the outset that this is a far more complex play than the preceding ones, and far more original in form vis-à-vis the bourgeois theatre of the turn of the century. This is the first of a group of plays (including *Each in His Own Way*, *Tonight We Improvise*, and, possibly, *The Mountain Giants*) in which Pirandello deals with the art of the theatre. The theme of the nature of artistic creation, of the relationship between art and everyday reality, touched upon only incidentally in previous plays, is explored here for the first time. The staging of a play, and even the process of its creation, is put on stage. The themes, the plots, all the familiar conventions (including the use of the scenic space) of the bourgeois theatre – still employed, albeit with subversive intent, in *Right You Are* – are utterly rejected. It is a revolutionary play, and it was perceived as such when it was first performed on 10 May 1921 at the Valle Theatre in Rome, and later in Milan, Paris, and throughout the world, where it was justly to become Pirandello's best-known play.

The concept of such a play had been evolving in Pirandello's mind for a long time. In the 'Preface' to the play he describes the birth of the characters from the author's imagination:

For many years now ... a nimble little servant ... called imagination ... has been in the employment of my art ...; she enjoys bringing home, for me to derive stories and novels and plays from, the most disgruntled characters in the world ... entangled in strange situations from which they cannot find a way out, thwarted in their dreams, cheated in their hopes – with whom, in short, it is often painful to deal. ('Preface' to *Six Characters*, I 34)

In an earlier short story, he had revealed the process by which the characters evolve in the author's mind, acquiring vitality and autonomy:

It has been an old custom of mine to give audience every Sunday morning to the characters of my future stories. Five hours, from 8:00 am. to 1:00 pm.

I almost always find myself in bad company. I do not know why the world's most discontented people usually come to these receptions of mine, or people afflicted by strange illnesses, or tangled up in the strangest sort of affairs, and it is really painful to deal with them.

I listen to them with great forbearance; I question them quite kindly; I take note of their names and the situation each one is in; I register their feelings and their aspirations. But I must add that, unfortunately for me, I am not easily satisfied. Forbearance, kindness, yes; but I do not like being conned. I want to delve deeply into their souls through a long and subtle inquiry.[1]

Finally, when through that process they had become 'alive to the point that you could touch them, so alive that you could feel their breathing' (I 36) – when, that is, their drama had acquired sufficient solidity and truth – then Pirandello would begin to give it form in a short story, novel, or play.

One such group of characters, born of the author's imagination and developed to the point of being charged with a kind of independent life – although, not having been given definitive artistic form, they are unfinished, in flux – is the group of six about whom Pirandello wrote to his son Stefano, a prisoner of war, in 1917: 'six characters involved in a terrible drama or tragedy who are following me everywhere because they want to get into a novel; a real obsession; but I say no, no, to them, that it is useless, that they do not interest me, that nothing interests me anymore, and they show me their wounds and I chase them away.'[2]

Although they have not yet received definitive artistic form, they already have a drama, a drama that makes them dramatic characters: 'To exist, every creature of the imagination, every artistic character, must have its drama, the drama in which and thanks to which it is a character. Its drama is a character's *raison d'être*, its vital function, essential to its existence' ('Preface' to *Six Characters*, I 40). The six characters' ruling passion is that drama; it colours their vision of reality, conditions their thoughts and their behaviour, torments them, enslaves them, obsesses them – turns them, that is, into dramatic characters.

Unfortunately, the drama in which they *think* they are characters resembles too closely in plot and spirit certain late-nineteenth-century romantic plays, especially the bourgeois theatre of the turn of the century:

A wealthy, self-styled intellectual makes the gesture of reaching out for 'normalcy' by marrying an ordinary woman. A son is born, and the father immediately delivers him to a healthy country nurse to raise; while the mother, unoccupied in the large house, seems more able to communicate with the husband's down-to-earth secretary than with the husband himself. The latter, noticing their affinity, decides to rid himself of his wife by favouring their union. The two set up house in another part of town; soon a daughter is born. The Father keeps an eye on the new family for a while. Occasionally he meets the Stepdaughter on her way home from school and presses some little present on her, which arouses suspicion in the parents, who move away leaving no trace behind. Unfortunately the secretary dies – some years and two more children later – and poverty takes his place. The Mother brings the family back and takes in sewing jobs for a modiste, Madame Pace, who behind her workshop runs a secret house of prostitution. Every time the Stepdaughter, now eighteen, comes to deliver her mother's work, Madame Pace complains about the quality of the work and cuts the payment, while trying to make her understand that both complaints and cuts would cease if she would lend herself to Madame's other business. The Stepdaughter agrees in order to save her mother constant humiliation. And one day one of Madame Pace's clients is the now fiftyish Father; his attempts to undress the Stepdaughter are interrupted by the Mother, whose suspicions about her daughter's fate have brought her to the atelier to put an end to the sordid trafficking. The Father, having thus rediscovered the little family, takes them out of the squalor of their rented room and brings them home. Here, however, the first son, now twenty-two, decides to treat the Mother he has never known and the bastards who have invaded his home with 'sullen indifference' and the Father, the author of such surprises, with 'repressed anger' (I 55). The one who suffers most intensely from this rejection is the Mother, and the intensity of her grief is felt by the two younger children as if through physical contact; they clutch her hands constantly without uttering a word, observing everything with wide eyes. Finally the intensity of the gnawing torment they sense in their mother overcomes them. The girl drowns herself in the garden fountain and the boy shoots himself. While the Mother continues to pursue her first son from room to room, 'her arms stretched out to him' (I 116), imploring understanding, the older daughter leaves to become a streetwalker.

While the characters call this 'a painful drama' on various occasions (e.g., I 56, 57), their author has evidently seen it for what it is, something of an old-fashioned tearjerker, material typical of the bourgeois theatre, the kind of literature that Pirandello rejected from the very beginning of his career as a playwright. (To the Father who suspects that perhaps the author has rejected them because of the Stepdaughter's importunity ['Perhaps it was because of you; because of your inordinate insistence, your inordinate excesses!'], she says: 'Most certainly not! He made me the way I am! I think instead he was disheartened, scornful of the theatre, as the public usually thinks of it and likes it,' I 106.) Therefore, no matter how often and insistently they have come back to their sessions with the author, trying to persuade him ('What we are doing before you, we have done again and again before him, trying to convince him, ... in the melancholy of that study of his, at dusk, when, slouched in his easy chair, he could not make up his mind to turn the light on and he let the darkness invade the room, teeming with us, who came to tempt him ... What scenes we came to propose to him!' I 105–6), the author has decided not to write a story or a novel or a play about them, not to set down in a text or give definitive form to these characters and to their drama ('The author who created us, live, then refused to, or physically could not, bring us into the world of art,' I 58).

And they resent that denial, because definitive artistic form would have meant not just the gift of life, but also immortality:

> It was a real crime ... because he who has the good fortune to be born a live character can laugh even at death. He will never die! The person, the writer, the tool of creation will die; his creature will never die! And to live forever one does not require extraordinary gifts, one needn't perform miracles. Who was Sancho Panza? Who was Don Abbondio? Yet they live for-

ever, because – live seeds – they had the good fortune to find a fertile
matrix, an imagination that was able to raise and nourish them, make
them live forever! (I 58–9)

They must instead be content with having been made live characters
– but characters, not people, and a character is a creature of the imagination, a form of communication that lives only in the act of communicating ('We, as characters, have no reality outside this illusion ... What
for you is an illusion to create, for us is our only reality,' I 102–3).

In order to live, therefore, these characters, rejected by their creator
and thus deprived of a desirable immortal life, are in search of any
occasion to communicate, that is, to live, even if only for a moment: a
compromise, to be sure, with immortality, but certainly better than
nothingness ('We want to live, sir, ... if only for a moment,' I 59). Paying
a visit to an acting company engaged in a rehearsal might just do the
trick; if they were allowed to act out the play they carry inside them,
they would live for at least that moment; and when they realize that the
prompter might put down their part in shorthand, they even begin to
think that the director might take the place of the author, put together a
script, give them definitive artistic form, and with it the immortality
their creator denied them.

But they must soon realize that without definitive artistic form it is
nearly impossible for them to communicate, that is, to live, even for just
a moment. In the absence of a script, they are almost unable to communicate their drama, to develop their play for their audience; they can do
it only in fragments, and primarily through narrative rather than dramatic scenes. Even the two dramatic scenes they try to put together are
not successful: the seduction scene, constantly interrupted by external
distractions, seems to the characters to lose all its dramatic power when
the actors give their unsatisfactory performance; and the final scene,
which is extremely short, produces chaos and rejection, instead of
understanding and acceptance, and puts an end to the characters' illusion that they might get some help from this theatrical company in
achieving their goal.

Dramatic art is uniquely subject to betrayals along the winding path
that leads from the initial inspiration to the artist's text, to a director's
interpretation, to that of the acting company, and finally to the audience's perception, when the text actually exists; imagine then when it is
absent. Thus, the disappointment of the six characters when they see
themselves so poorly interpreted by the actors is enormous: 'Would

you be able to live in front of a mirror which not only freezes us with our own image, but sends it back to us with a grimace that is an unrecognizable distortion of ourselves?' (I 113).

The very nature of this particular theatrical company further complicates things. It is a company accustomed to perform conventional, sentimental, romantic, simplistic plays of the turn-of-the-century bourgeois theatre ('What can I do if we don't get any good plays from France any more?' the Director complains, I 53), a company that cannot even begin to understand the new 'Pirandellian' theatre:

> ... and we're reduced to staging Pirandello's, which nobody understands, purposely written to leave actors, critics, and public eternally dissatisfied? Yes, a chef's hat! And beat those eggs! Do you think those eggs you're beating are all there is to it? No! You've got to portray the shell of the eggs you're beating! ... That is, the empty form of reason without the content of blind instinct! You are reason, your wife instinct, in a game of assigned roles, in which you who are acting out your role are intentionally playing the puppet of yourself. Understand?
> *The leading actor (with a gesture of resignation)*: No, I don't.
> *The Director*: Neither do I! (I 53)

Thus, on the one hand, director and actors become interested in the family drama of the six characters ('I assure you that all this interests me very, very much. I feel, intuitively, that there is material here for a beautiful play,' the Director says, I 75), since it is the very stuff of turn-of-the-century, bourgeois, sentimental theatre; but on the other hand they will never understand the complex nature of these 'characters,' the problems they embody as 'characters.' They will even mistake them for 'persons' who, having lived their strange story in real life, now want to put it on the stage for some hidden exhibitionistic or financial reason (so that when the Mother becomes agitated and refuses to leave when the scene in the rear of Madame Pace's atelier is being readied, the Director will try to calm her down by reminding her that this is only a play and not the past experience of her real life: 'Hasn't all this already taken place in the past?! I don't understand you!' And, of course, he will not understand the Mother's cry of protest: 'No, it's taking place now; it's always taking place! My torment isn't over, sir! I'm alive and present, always, in every moment of my torment, which recreates itself, alive and present, always,' I 99). For the acting company, the different nature of the characters, their differing consciousness of being 'characters' and not persons, or of having a role in their play, will remain a mystery.

While 'the Father and the Stepdaughter ... more than the others are aware of being characters' (I 40), not persons, creatures of art in search of the moment of life that they can have only by communicating, the Mother has no awareness of acting a role; she lives and suffers it as a person in real life would, the way the creature of art she is not aware of being must; she lives 'the eternal moment' (I 99) each time she is compelled to act the play with her family; for her it is always the first time. While the suffering of the characters who are aware of being characters seems somewhat diminished thanks to their cathartic awareness, hers is as urgent as that of a real person. Whereas the Father and the Stepdaughter, conscious of the fact that, as characters, they live only by communicating, 'obviously are more forthcoming and lead and almost drag along the dead weight of the others' (I 39), the Mother

> does not care at all about living ... she has no doubt whatsoever about being alive; nor has the need to ask herself how and why she is alive ever crossed her mind. She has no consciousness of being a character since she is never, not even for a second, detached from her 'role' ... she lives in a continuity of feeling that knows no interruption; thus she cannot become aware of the nature of her life, that is, of her being a character. ('Preface' to *Six Characters*, I 41–2)

The nature of her two children whose hands she is clasping is very similar to hers; they experience through that contact her own unsettling emotions. The Son, instead, keeps denying that he is a character, that he has a drama; the others might, he does not, he has no role to play in their drama, the author did not assign him one and he will not play one:

> I've got no role in it and I don't want to have any; you know that I'm not cut out to have any place among you people! ... My feelings cannot produce any action on my part ... I am an 'unrealized' character, dramatically, and I feel uneasy, downright ill in their company. (I 73–4)

The six characters are different ('Apparently not all six characters have reached the same degree of evolution') both because 'among them some are primary, some are secondary figures, that is "protagonists" and mere "presences" – which is basic perspective, necessary to any theatrical or narrative structure'; and because they must perform different functions, that is, they are 'all ... completely formed,' but only for the 'end each serves' ('Preface' to *Six Characters*, I 39). Certainly their most striking difference is their differing awareness of their nature as characters and the needs inherent in that nature: needs they all feel, but of which they are not all equally aware and to satisfy which, therefore, they do not all struggle with the same intelligence and sense of urgency.

As characters in their turn-of-the-century sentimental family melodrama, they were rejected by their creator, who did not cast their story in definitive artistic form. But while rejecting them as characters in that tearful bourgeois play, he cast them in another play, a deeper, more modern play, the play of the rejected characters in search of an author, whose real drama is the need and the difficulty of human communication ('One must understand what part of them I refused: not them, of course, but their drama, which, no doubt, interested them above all, not me,' 'Preface' to *Six Characters*, I 40). Each to differing degrees of awareness, the six are conscious of being rejected characters in search of an author, but they must not discover that this, and not their cheap family drama, is their real drama. Even as they are in desperate search of their author and feeling deeply the deprivation inflicted on them, they must continue to believe that the drama that makes them characters, creatures of art, potentially capable of achieving immortality, is the family drama that did not get written and that they want to act out; because if they were to discover that the drama that makes them immortal is instead their search for an author, and that the definitive artistic form they are seeking has been granted them in this 'other' play, they would stop worrying about rejection, they would stop searching for their author, they would cease to exist as characters in this play, and this play would no longer exist.

Instead, conscious of both rejection and search, but unconscious that their real drama consists precisely in this situation, the six characters live this drama with the passion with which any authentic character must live its drama ('the drama in which and thanks to which he is a character,' I 40). *And it is in the passionate experience of this drama in which they do not know that they are characters* – the drama of being rejected characters, unwilling to be deprived of the most powerful form of communication, of definitive artistic form and ultimately of immortality – *and not in the presentation of their family drama, that they develop and express the complex Pirandellian themes of this play.* This is accomplished both in their collective effort to project their family drama as an interesting one so that the Director and his actors may allow them to act it out, so that it may be put down in shorthand – in short, in their *collective effort to find an author*, to give form to their formless drama – and in the individual effort of each character to make its own idea of the drama prevail, to influence the final shape of the script, if one is to be produced, as far as it can – again, in their *individual effort to find an author* ('He wants to go straight to performing his "inner torment"; but I want to put on my drama! mine!' says the Stepdaughter, protesting the inordinate input of the Father; 'You can't have one character coming forward that much, upstaging everybody else, taking over the stage,' the Director warns her, I 97).

The language of the play reflects the distinction between the two dramatizations. Being an old-fashioned, turn-of-the-century melodrama, the family drama is presented in the familiar naturalistic language of the bourgeois theatre; when the characters are revealing the background of their family drama, their individual passions, their part in that drama, and acting out the two scenes they succeed in staging, they use this language consistently and insist on 'realistic' staging:

> *The Stepdaughter*: O Lord, sir, she told me what you already know: that my mother's work was badly done again; that the material's wasted; and that I must be understanding if I want her to go on helping us in our poverty. (I 87)

> No, no, my dear sir! He's got to tell me what he told me: 'Then, let's get rid of this nice little dress right away!' And I, with all that mourning in my heart, only two months old, I went over there, see? behind that screen, and with these fingers shaking with shame and revulsion, I unhooked my corset, my dress ... (I 96–7)

The Director and his actors too, accustomed as they are to bourgeois comedies or romantic dramas, French or Italian, speak, as we have heard, in the same naturalistic language:

> *The Director*: What can I do if we don't get any good plays from France any more? And we're reduced to staging Pirandello's, which nobody understands, purposely written to leave actors, critics, and public eternally dissatisfied? (I 53);

or, when they try to move beyond their limitations and talk about the new theatre, they parody a critical language that is incomprehensible to them:

The Director: Do you think those eggs you're beating are all there is to it? No! You've got to portray the shell of the eggs you're beating! ... That is, the empty form of reason without the content of blind instinct! You are reason, your wife instinct, in a game of assigned roles, in which you who are acting out your role are intentionally playing the puppet of yourself. Understand?
The leading actor (with a gesture of resignation): No, I don't.
The Director: Neither do I! (I 53)

But the language of the play alters when the six characters interrupt the presentation of their family drama and take on the role of 'Pirandellian' characters in search of understanding from their uncomprehending audience (the Director and his actors). They become characters trying to explain their essence as creations of art, imagined by their author and rejected, cast into the limbo of formlessness, deprived of an immortality they feel is their due, despairing, like Dante's souls in limbo who 'without hope, live in desire,' of ever obtaining the immortality of art. And as soon as, fired by this passion, they assume this role, their language rises to new levels of conceptual coherence, capable of expressing the awareness of the artist, the mystery of artistic creation, and the problems of its genesis, of its translation into formal expression, of its communication to an audience:

You know very well that life is full of endless absurdities which – shamelessly – don't even need to look realistic, because they're real ... that it might really be crazy to try to do the contrary – that is, to try to create realistic ones which look real; but ... if it's crazy, it's also the only reason for your craft ...: to give life on the stage to ... living beings, more alive than those who breathe and wear clothes! Less real, perhaps, but truer to life! ... Nobody knows better than you that nature uses the human imagination as a tool to carry on its creative work on a higher level ... Aren't you accustomed to seeing them up here – alive, confronting each other, the characters created by an author? ... Believe us, we are really six characters, and extremely interesting ones! even if we are lost ... in the sense that the author who created us, live, then refused to, or physically could not, bring us into the world of art. And it was a real crime, sir, because he who has the good fortune to be born a live character can laugh even at death. He will never die! The person, the writer, the tool of creation will die; his creature will never die! And to live forever one does not require extraordinary gifts, one needn't perform miracles. Who was Sancho Panza? Who was Don Abbondio? Yet they live forever, because – live seeds – they had the good fortune to find a fertile matrix, an imagination that was able to raise and nourish them, make them live forever! (I 56–9)

It is a language capable of dealing with complex problems of poetics and aesthetics with clarity and force. To the Director who interjects, 'I'd like to know when a character has ever been seen stepping out of his role and speaking for it, defending it, explaining it, the way you're doing?' the Father replies that a 'live character' possesses autonomy, vitality, an expressive life of its own:

You've never seen it because authors usually don't disclose the laborious process of creation. Yet if the characters are alive, really alive, before their author, he does nothing but observe the words, the gestures, they suggest to him; he must want them the way they want themselves to be; he has to! When a character is born, he immediately acquires such independence even from his author that he can be imagined by everybody in situations in which his author never thought of putting him, and takes on a significance, at times, that his author never dreamed of giving him! ... So why wonder at us? Think of the bad luck of a character born, alive, as I said, from the imagination of an author, who then wanted to deny him life, and tell me if this character, left as he is, alive and deprived of life, has no business doing what we're doing before you now, after having done it again and again before him, believe me, in order to convince him, to push him – sometimes me, sometimes the girl, sometimes that poor mother ... (I 105)

A character is endowed, the Father asserts, with a permanence that people whose reality is in constant flux cannot enjoy:

A character really has a life of his own, distinguished by qualities of his own, so that he's always 'someone.' While a man ... may be 'nobody' ... Only to find out if you, as you are now, really see yourself as you now see for instance, from a distance, what you once were, with all the illusions you had then, with all the things, inside and outside of you, the way they seemed to you then – and were, really were for you –. Well, sir, thinking of all those illusions long gone, of all the things that no longer 'seem' to you the way they 'were' then, don't you feel ... the ground itself giving way under your feet, realizing that in the same way 'everything' that is real for you today, is bound to reveal itself an illusion tomorrow? ... Your reality can change from one day to the next, ... ours doesn't ... it can't change, or be different, ever, because it's been fixed – this way – 'this one' – forever –

... Our unchangeable reality should make you shudder when you come close to us! (I 104–5)

The reality of the character consists only in the illusion created by the work of art; it lives only in the crucial moment of communication:

The Father: Here, for you and your actors, it's simply a matter ... of a game ... the game of your craft, which has to create a perfect illusion of reality ... We, as characters, have no reality outside this illusion! ... What for you is an illusion to create, for us is our only reality! (I 102–3)

The Stepdaughter [talking to her little sister]: A stage is a place where you play at being serious ... It may be a game for others, but not for you, unfortunately, you who are real ... and are playing for real in a real pool. (I 111)

The Mother [to the Director, who thinks she is replaying her past]: No, it's taking place now, it's always taking place! My torment isn't over, sir! I'm alive and present, always, in every moment of my torment, which recreates itself, alive and present, always. But those two little children ... keep clutching my hands to keep my torment alive and present ... And this one ... if I see her here before me, it's for the same purpose ... to recreate, alive and present, the torment I felt for her too!
The Father: The eternal moment, as I told you, sir! (I 99)

It is only as we reflect on the text that we realize how effectively this language deals with complex aesthetic questions, because as it is spoken by the characters it demonstrates the dynamism, the immediacy, the vivid imagery of animated conversation. The conceptual discourse is punctuated by frequent exclamations ('There you are! Exactly! To living beings, more alive than those who breathe and wear clothes! Less real, perhaps, but truer to life! We share the same opinion!' I 57; 'But this is where the root of all evil lies! in words! We all carry a world of things inside of us; each a world of his own!' I 65), ellipses ('But, but ... you just said ...' I 57; 'But if you really can change from one day to the next ...' I 105), and rhetorical questions ('But what do you really mean to say?' I 57; 'But those two little children, have you heard them speak?' I 99; 'Illusion? Please, don't say illusion,' I 102; 'We have no reality outside this illusion! Yes, gentlemen! What other reality can we have?' I 103; 'Would you be able to tell me who you are?' ibid.), by numerous interjections and vocatives ('eh,' 'sir,' 'yes sir,' 'see,' 'please,' 'I beg you,' 'nothing, sir,' 'just so, sir,' 'no, what on earth are you saying, sir,' 'no, pardon me, I was thinking about you, sir,' 'but allow me to remind you that ...'). These devices produce the feeling of immediacy proper to lively dialogue, as do the frequent interruptions in the flow of the speech by parenthetical expressions ('a man – I am not saying you, necessarily – a man in general may be "nobody,"' I 104; 'But ours doesn't, sir! Don't you see? This is the difference! It doesn't change, it can't change, or be different, ever, because it's been fixed – this way – "this one" – forever – (it is a terrible thing, sir!) our unchangeable reality ...' I 195), and by punctuation that conceals the length of a highly hypotactic sentence ('It's true, sir, I too, I came too, to try to convince him, many times, in the melancholy of that studio of his, at dusk, when, slouched in his easy chair, he couldn't make up his mind to turn the light on and he let the darkness invade the room, darkness teeming with us, who came to tempt him ...' I 105–6). The speech of the Mother, the most instinctual of the six characters, who must, however, express the difficult idea of the eternal actuality of her torment, is broken into very short sentences, explosive fragments of thought expressed almost exclusively through exclamations, a sequence of short, sharp cries of grief ('No, it's taking place now, it's always taking place! My torment isn't over, sir! I'm alive and present, always, in every moment of my torment, which recreates itself, alive and present, always,' I 99).

Although these might at first appear mere rhetorical devices, their effect is in fact highly dramatic. Pirandello's extraordinary stylistic inventiveness makes the difference between the static, abstract discourse that deadens so many twentieth-century plays[3] and a dramatic interaction full of colour and energy, explosions of thought, passionate and magnificently eloquent characters.

Another important Pirandellian technique that keeps the development of these themes from abstraction is the pervasive use of images, references, and examples that are immediate and concrete. Thus, the Father's statement: 'We are here in search of an author' (I 55), to express the characters' sense of their lack of definitive artistic form and their quest for it; his comparison of the reality of the creations of art to that of living persons: 'living beings, more alive than those who breathe and wear clothes' (I 57); his explanation of a distinction between the creation of a character and its definitive artistic expression: 'the author who created us, live, then refused to ... bring us into the world of art' (I 58). The concrete examples of Sancho Panza and Don Abbondio corroborate the achievement of immortality: 'he who has the good fortune to be born a live character can laugh even at death. He will never die!' (I 58). Complaining in very plain language ('and how can we understand each other, sir, if in the words I use I put the meaning and value of things as they are within me,' I 65) of the inadequacy of words to express one's own reality, the Father turns for corroboration to the concrete example before him: 'Look, my pity, all my pity for this woman (*points to the Mother*) she takes as the direst cruelty' (I 65–6). Lamenting the inadequacy of the perception of others regarding an individual who is aware of being 'one' and 'many' ('"one" with this person, "another" with that, all very different! And we have the illusion, meanwhile, that we're always being "the same for everyone,"' I 72), and the fact that other people, and even works of art, can reduce the multiplicity of an individual to a single dimension ('we realize it very well, when in one of our acts, by a most unfortunate accident, we remain suddenly suspended as from a hook: we realize, that is, that not all of ourselves is in that act,' I 72–3), he refers again to the concrete example before him:

Now do you understand the malice of this young woman? She caught me in a place, in an act, in which she shouldn't have met me ... and she wants to stick me with an identity I never dreamed I could take on for her, in a fleeting, shameful moment of my life. (I 73)

She is here to capture me, freeze me, keep me hooked and suspended for eternity, pilloried, in that single fleeting and shameful moment of my life. (I 99)

The Mother as well, speaking about her 'torment which renews itself, alive and present, always,' gives concreteness to its reality by calling the attention of her audience to its concrete consequences, in the silence and staring eyes of the two children who clutch her hands and share her torment through that contact: 'But those two little children, have you heard them speak? They can no longer speak, sir! They keep on clutching my hands to keep my torment alive and present, but they in themselves no longer exist!' (I 99).

The language of the Son, too, exemplifies the concrete imagery that pervades all the 'conceptual' passages of this play. For instance, to tell the Director that it is impossible to communicate with exactitude, without falsification, the essence of an artistic character, he shouts at him: 'But haven't you understood that you can't perform this play? We are not inside you, and your actors are looking at us from the outside' (I 113). And to explain the revulsion that seizes the dramatic characters and their author when they see themselves betrayed by the interpretation of a poor theatrical company, he uses the familiar image of a mirror in a novel way: 'Would you be able to live in front of a mirror which not only freezes us with our own image, but sends it back to us with a grimace that's an unrecognizable distortion of ourselves?' (I 113).

We have, then, two types of language: the familiar, naturalistic language in which the characters present their family drama, and the conceptual one in which the characters define their essence as creations of art and live their role as characters in search of an author. Yet we find the transition between one and the other almost imperceptible. In vivid immediacy and inventive power, the conceptual language matches and indeed surpasses the other. The six characters in search of an author live their quest for life, if not immortality, as forcefully, as passionately, as the six characters who play out their family melodrama. The search for communication and for life is more imperative, truer to life, than the naturalistic play within the play. And it is, as we have noted, when the characters live their 'role' as characters, aware of the possibility of definitive artistic form, aggrieved at not having achieved it, searching for a way to communicate their drama, rather than in the presentation of the family drama itself, that the new themes of the Pirandellian theatre are developed.

Pirandello himself in his post-preface gives us the essence of the major themes:

> The delusion of mutual understanding, irremediably based on the empty abstraction of words; the multiple personality of every individual, deriving from all the possibilities of being present in each one of us; and finally the inherent, tragic conflict between life that constantly moves and changes, and form which fixes it immutably. ('Preface' to *Six Characters*, I 38)

Beneath these themes lies the larger, inclusive one of the human need for communication and the difficulty, if not the impossibility, of satisfying it. To convey one's own individual human reality is rendered difficult both by the inescapable subjectivity of one's own perception of oneself and the reality around one, and by the very nature of language itself. 'But this is where the root of all evil lies! in words! ... We think we understand each other, but we never do!' (I 65), complains the Father at the conclusion of a long dispute with his Stepdaughter and the Director in which this idea is developed, arising from the attempt by each character to promote its own view of the events.

And this is a difficulty that not even communication through achieved artistic form can escape. The creation of imagination, the 'live character,' might have 'the good fortune to find,' besides a creator, 'a fertile matrix, an imagination able to raise and nourish' it, make it 'live forever' (I 58–9), bring it, that is, from the original conception to the definitive formal stage not impoverished, diminished, frozen, but richly and fully realized, so that its betrayal by future interpreters will be more difficult. Yet inevitably that definitive artistic form would be subject to endless interpretive betrayals in the moment of communication, since each interpreter brings to it a whole world of ideas and feelings, a personal sensibility that is never exactly that of the author. Language is always tied to the subjectivity of the communicants. And drama is more than any other art form at the mercy of this subjectivity, given the series of interpreters it must go through, from author to director, to actors, to audience. The six characters, unable to hide their disappointment at the interpretation of their drama by the acting company, are led to understand this clearly.

But in addition to their complaint about the interpretive shortcomings of the actors, the six characters are also aware that the definitive artistic form they pursue so intelligently and persistently will never succeed in rendering wholly the multiplicity of the individual, nor the flow, the dynamic pulse, of real life; art will tend to freeze, to contract, to simplify life. At the very moment we think we have succeeded in capturing life, it is already evolving into something different – a truth Pirandello had found in Vico: 'I cling to the belief that I am always the same; yet the constant approach and departure of things that flow into and out of me, make me different every moment. More or less in the way in which movement that seems straight is subject to constant distortions.'[4]

The reality the artist has created is defined, finished, unchanging, while everyday reality is in continual flux – not to be captured, in this sense, by artistic form or by any form in which life may be frozen. Yet life itself, to escape the solitude of inarticulate chaos, is condemned to organize itself, to seek a form, by which it then feels it has been imprisoned or limited, and against which (like the Father contesting the role of seducer in which he is cast by the Stepdaughter) it eventually tries to rebel.

Human beings are always dissatisfied with these limitations, but in their irrepressible need to communicate and to be understood, they accept as inevitable the need for a crystallizing form, however inadequate, as the only means by which to reveal themselves to others. This is the central dramatic experience of these six Pirandellian characters, developed in all the encounters between them and the members of the acting company: to be 'in search of an author,' or definitive artistic form, as a necessary means to communication. And if definitive artistic form is not available, a compromise is certainly better than nothing: if not the immortality of the characters of the great masterpieces, at least the compromise of living even 'only for a moment' in the actors they chance upon – aware, after all, that even definitive artistic form would have been a compromise (albeit the best of compromises) with elusive reality. This is a thematic complex clearly developed while the characters live the role assigned to them by their author in this play – that of being in search of an author – and not while they narrate, a bit at a time, their family melodrama.

By using dramatic characters *as* characters Pirandello explores on another level a basic theme of all his work, the fundamental human need to communicate and the difficulty of satisfying it. For, however impoverished a human life may be without communication, the life of a character is literally entirely dependent on it: in a character, which is a means of communication and can live only in the act of communicating, the need to communicate is as imperious as the human urge to live.

5 The 'Powerful Logic' of *Henry IV*

> I do it as a game. You do it in earnest. But I assure you – no matter how in
> earnest you are – you too are wearing a disguise.
>
> <div align="right">(<i>Henry IV</i>, I 326)</div>

In his well-known and perceptive essay on 'The Theatre of Luigi Pirandello,' Adriano Tilgher concludes his discussion of *Henry IV* with the
observation that 'the structure of the tragedy is such that the stages of
its development ... pass before our eyes in a swift and relentless succession of scenes, bound together by a profound and powerful logic.'[1]
Tilgher's thorough knowledge of Pirandello's theatre and his keen
insight are uncommon, however, and audiences as well as critics of this
play have often failed to perceive the 'profound and powerful logic' of
its development, its thematic richness, and its greatness as a dramatic
work. Writing about the 1973 Broadway production of *Henry IV*, for
instance, Clive Barnes, in a tentative and cautiously laudatory review in
the *New York Times*, confessed that he felt as if he had been confronted
by an 'inspired Chinese puzzle.'[2] But his colleague Walter Kerr, with no
hesitation, accused those who praise the play of calling it a masterpiece
in order to avoid the task of analysing it and concluding otherwise; and
taking upon himself the task of analysing it, he concluded in no uncertain terms that *Henry IV* is an 'awkward, erratic' play, which 'never
seems to function as well on stage as, say *Six Characters in Search of an
Author* or even *Right You Are, if You Think You Are.*'[3]

It is the first act in particular that Kerr found 'awkward'; first, he
complained, we are given 'the circumstances of the play in an exposition so bold, so left-handed, so undramatized as to invite us to keep

scorecards ... and there is nothing to call this but clumsy,' and then the madman himself comes before us to illustrate 'what we have been told. The curtain falls on the first act without our having moved an inch, smelled a rat, been given a direction. Awkward indeed.' He labelled the entire development of the action 'erratic': 'What is erratic about the play is the dramatic abruptness.' Kerr pointed to the sudden twists and turns of the action: not only the killing of Belcredi at the end of the play, but in the very centre, the revelation, first to the councillors and later to the visitors, of Henry's regained sanity. The revelation to the latter group, particularly, 'is so abrupt as to make a man wonder why he bothered to establish the scene' (the first scene of the third act, that is, when the live characters take the place of the portraits, to produce the decisive therapeutic shock). 'What was to have been a key sequence has been washed away by a piece of offstage information, and we are plunged, willy-nilly, into open, contemporary conversation. As play-making, inexplicable,' lamented Kerr. Compelled to admit, however, that although certain aspects of the play are 'as frustrating as can be,' the spectator's interest never fades, he tried to explain the phenomenon by claiming that the fascination of this play lies in the felt presence of the author's intelligence: 'we respond not so much to the play as to the mind that could have conceived such a play ... we are still held to it by the magnet of an intelligence, a force felt even while we are faulting the craftsmanship.' Clearly we are not dealing with a masterpiece, he concluded: 'a masterpiece? No, I don't think so, not beside the mysteriously perfect interplay of thought and event in *Six Characters*.'[4]

It is a surprising conclusion for one who professes to recognize the thematic richness and stylistic perfection of *Six Characters* because in thematic complexity, stylistic originality, and dramatic structure *Henry IV* rivals *Six Characters* more closely than perhaps any other play by Pirandello; and because one who approaches *Henry IV* understanding the greatness of *Six Characters* should find it easier to perceive the greatness of this other masterpiece of Pirandello's maturity.

Let us first consider the thematic complexity of the play. *Henry IV*, like most of the author's major plays, centres around a 'Pirandellian' character, that is, a character tormented, persecuted, insulted by a philistine society that is insensitive and ignorantly self-assured, that makes its own laws and imposes them on everything. A society that makes arbitrary value judgments on individual behaviour, on human liberty, on the definition of sanity and madness. A complacent bourgeois society that thinks it is pursuing the common good by allowing the madman to hold court, while actually keeping him shut up as dangerous, and at most providing him with the 'help' of a scientific charlatan, to whom it accords authority and respect. A society in which Henry IV, a thinker, a poet, a serious man, hence 'a man of sorrow,' was therefore already considered quite strange, before the famous pageant – so strange that his supposed friends were led to play a joke on him that left him really mad, after which they felt justified at last in isolating him in the abyss of his misery.

It is clear, however, that Henry IV is seen throughout by his creator as more human than his enemies, because of his suffering and the penetration of his thought – an extraordinarily human, though solitary, hero. While in *Right You Are* and *Six Characters* a group of Pirandellian characters are misunderstood by a group of complacent bourgeois, here we have one man alone, as in some classical tragedies (Aeschylus' Prometheus, Sophocles' Philoctetes, etc.), condemned to experience the ingratitude and insensitivity of human society. He too is visited by those who think they are pursuing the common good, and are actually pursuing their own (particularly the two older lovers, the guilty original agents of Henry's tragedy, who privately hope that their responsibility may have been forgotten by the victim after so many years, just as they have done their best to forget it).

Henry IV is unlike the classical heroes, however, in that his relentless thought has led him to a characteristically modern, pessimistic appreciation of the absurdity of each man's illusion about his freedom and sanity. Before the tragic choice of surviving by compromising his nature as a hero and thus condemning himself to obscurity, or asserting his heroic nature even if it means physical death, the classical tragic hero chooses the heroic, tragic end. Henry IV – awakening with grey hair after so many years of darkness, clearly aware of the loss of twelve years of youth – is faced with the possibility of taking off the mask of insanity and re-entering everyday reality, of trusting himself to the casual surge of the instincts, the whirl of events, the chaos of human desires, to the mutable and uncontrollable life that his adversaries foolishly think they are able to control (and which will in fact betray him when for a moment he entrusts himself to it in the final part of the play). Confronting this possibility, he chooses survival. He chooses to control his world by continuing voluntarily to wear the mask that chance had imposed on him, the mask that the rest wear unawares.

His humanity does not suffer for this unheroic choice. His is not the heroic humanity of the protagonist of earlier tragedy, but that of a twentieth-century hero, akin to Mattia Pascal, or the characters of Svevo and other twentieth-century writers – vulnerable, unjustly excluded, driven to alienation. Nor does Henry's role as a main character suffer. He dominates this play just as much as Prometheus or Philoctetes – or Lear – do theirs. But although the author's celebration of a final, unrecognized wisdom acquired through the experience of profound suffering given witness in the play strongly recalls King Lear as well as Prometheus and Philoctetes, Henry IV is as different from the Shakespearean hero as he is from the heroes of Greek tragedy. His stature in this play in no way derives from the status of an emperor or king or prince who retains his essential majesty even when most deeply stricken by misfortune, nor is he attended by the sacred aura of heroes touched by fate or the furies, like Prometheus enchained, or Lear in the tempest, or Oedipus at Colonus. He dominates precisely in his character as an ordinary mortal, whose costume recalls if anything that of the Son of Man before Pilate; it is that of a mock emperor, of a man who has been beaten and insulted by a cruel joke, of a poor mortal who has looked into the depths of truth in a way others did not or could not, and who has found it frightening enough to shrink from it, as behooves a man who shares our common weakness – the very opposite of the exceptional heroism of the protagonist of earlier tragedy.

And if Henry knows that he has behaved like a weak human being, he also knows that everyone wears a mask for the same reason and for the same purpose, even if unknowingly, and thus faults him unjustly for his weakness. Hence he is trying to open their eyes to their own hypocrisy, and they resent him for it and try to shut him up again, calling him insane. Yet the only means remaining to him to fight his persecutors is the strength of his passionate thought, his passionate search for truth that may explain and authenticate his suffering – suffering that society, far from recognizing in itself and pitying, scorns and rejects as illness, as an inhuman thing (I 309–15). The entire play underscores this search for and achievement of consciousness; it is pre-eminently a drama of awareness. Henry's drama lies not so much in the loss of the best years of his manhood (I 365), but in the understanding of the meaning of that loss (I 366); the author is placing before us not the diversion and suspense of a simulated madness, but a person's acquisition of the frightening awareness of the true essence of madness and sanity, as well as of their interrelationship in the views and behaviour of society present and past: 'it would be terrible for you to dwell, as I have, on this dreadful thing which can really drive a man insane' (I 353).

This society derides his consciously chosen assumption of a mask while unwittingly wearing a mask of its own: 'Hasn't it ever happened to you, my lady? ... But I assure you – no matter how in earnest you are – you too are wearing a disguise' (I 325–6); it derides the assumption of a mask as if the deception consciously devised in order to escape insanity were not a serious business and certainly more justifiable than the one its members wear perhaps for the same purpose, although unawares (I 368). It is a society that refuses to understand the depth of his tragedy and the excusable nature of his decision, when he reveals that he has regained sanity, and accuses him of playing a joke on it, and especially on those in it who at the pageant had played the cruel joke on him that cost him twelve years of his youth (I 365). It is a society that pretends to be free and in control of reality (I 325), while it is actually controlled by many things: by the uncontrollable events of life – birth, illness, death ('no one is willing to recognize that mysterious and inevitable power which limits our will,' I 324); by social conventions that dictate dress and behaviour; by the recluse himself whom they want to control and lock up as insane and who continually shows them that they are controlled by him, shaking like reeds before him (I 348–9). He is there, in fact, to shake the world ordered by their bourgeois sanity – hence their attempts, however useless, to keep him shut up and unheard, or to keep calling him insane, which should achieve the same effect (I 351–2).

Certainly he is given several chances to choose: ten years earlier when he had regained sanity, he had chosen to fake a continuing insanity; towards the end of the second act he chooses to reveal his sanity; after the killing of Belcredi (which is not a choice but an instinctual reaction brought on by a fit of blinding rage) he will have to choose again whether to go on faking insanity or to face the consequences of his action as a sane man. But each time it is the conscious choice of a man who has learned a terrible wisdom from the spectacle of a world seen from eight centuries away (I 354–5). While all the others, then, have one name in everyday life and another name in the historical travesty of the visit, because they are immersed in their unconscious doubleness, Henry IV is always the same intense, deeply serious man who both before and after the fall can stare into the depths of human feelings and draw back disconcerted, appalling everyone (I 312, 366). Even when he temporarily abandons his deception, except for an instant of blinding rage, his awareness does not diminish. He is not the common man of his time, and therefore does not bear a contemporary name. He has the consciousness and the experience of a historical character who can judge the world of the present, see the reality of the human predicament, from the rich experience of eight centuries of history (I 355). Even the historical Henry had made, and paid for, his mistakes, but he had understood his world and been able to wear the mask of the penitent to achieve his long-term goal, to survive as emperor; so too, the Pirandellian Henry, who has penetrated the essence of the common masquerade, understands his own conscious assumption of a mask.

If we accept the suggestion of Orazio Costa, a director who has had to contend more than once with this drama, that the form of *Henry IV* attempts to parody the court ambiance and the political intrigues of the historical melodramas so dear to turn-of-the-century audiences[5] (another possible parallel of the many between this play and *Right You Are* and *Six Characters*, in which both the physical and social environment and the staging of turn-of-the-century plays are ridiculed), it should be understood that in caricaturing a popular form of escapist theatre, this play underlines its own nature as a drama of modern and 'Pirandellian' consciousness.

However, Costa's idea that the 'visitors are clearly conceived as' a group of characters in a 'pochade,'[6] a type of turn-of-the-century French comedy centring on risqué situations, is certainly unacceptable. We have here, instead, one of those ingenious and typically Pirandellian refractions of parallel or contrasting characters and situations – already found in *Six Characters* and later more amply developed in *Each in His Own Way* – seen here in the reality of daily life, in the conscious and unconscious masquerade of the present and in that of twenty-two years earlier, as well as in the artistic representation of both reality and masquerade.

And as in *Six Characters*, here too the typically Pirandellian multiple refraction of the meanings of the various dramatic configurations demonstrates the singular ability of drama, and of Pirandellian theatre in particular, to look at reality from a position of detachment, more conducive to the discovery of its dramatic truth than the position of those who are immersed in life itself, and thus to the creation of persons and situations 'less real, perhaps, but truer.' The Henry IV who explains to his councillors the advantage of contemplating the maddening spectacle of twentieth-century humanity from the distance of eight centuries and seeing its falseness, its vanity, its misery, its insanity, is proposing that they do exactly what the dramatist tries to do and leads his audience to do through his play. Contemporary life is seen as an unintelligible and uncontrollable agony, because it is in flux, it is becoming; history is seen as an extraordinarily orderly universe, knowable because it is completed, fixed, as the completed work of art was seen in *Six Characters.*

In the latter play, however, the characters complain about its fixity even as they consider the completed work necessary to their survival, to their possible immortality as the creations of art, exactly as Henry recognizes that the niche he has chosen within the fixity of history is a means of survival, a wise choice, but still a bitter, unavoidable compromise. 'One is forced,' as Tilgher puts it, 'to give oneself a Form that one can never be satisfied with, because always, sooner or later, Life pays for the Form it has given itself or has let others impose on it; and in this clash between Life and the Form into which the individual has channelled it or others have channelled it for him, we find the essence of the theatre of Pirandello.'[7]

Henry IV equals *Six Characters* and the other masterpieces of Pirandello's maturity not only in thematic richness, but in the extraordinarily organic development of its action and the complex rhythm of its dramatic tension. The plot develops in an extremely effective and original way. On a decisively important visit to the 'mad' Henry, friends and relatives are accompanied by a psychiatrist, who is supposed to observe the 'madman' and explore the possibility of a cure, and who at a certain point believes he has found a stratagem that should snap the sick man out of his insanity. The first act, traditionally devoted to the establishment of the background of the situation, is divided in three parts: the first, on the pretext of the installation of a new councillor, reveals to the audience the present state of the 'madman'; the second, on the pretext of providing the doctor with basic information, gives the audience all the antecedents of the present situation; the third constitutes the first direct contact of the new councillor, the doctor, and the audience with the main character, an exploratory contact. Traditionally the second act is supposed to move the situation towards the definitive dramatic event that explodes at the beginning of the third act, followed by the gradual and successful resolution of all unresolved points. In Pirandello's second act, instead, purposes cross. While the doctor thinks up and readies his plan, the 'madman' (as later we realize we should have expected all along, given his absolute mastery of the situation) has matured his own plan, which, though at first it seems only to advance the doctor's by one scene, in fact thwarts it in the third act, and with it the goal of the visit itself. Resolutely and irrevocably, since it is sealed by the death of the most guilty of the visiting friends, Henry IV's plan effects a solution once again of his own choosing, rather than someone else's, although once again it is a bitter choice.

The development is not at all 'erratic,' as it has been called, but ingenious, and very characteristically Pirandellian, as characteristic as the rhythm of the dramatic tension effected by Pirandello with an extreme economy of means, making it coincide more or less with the tension and fear that the dominating hero of this play arouses in the other characters and, empathetically, in the audience.

The first scene of *Henry IV* has a comic tone that seems to put the audience at ease. But as the scene progresses we realize that the comedy of the councillors is rather macabre, and begin to feel the same uneasiness experienced by Berthold, the new councillor, as he becomes aware of the real nature of his new job. The strangeness of the situation has by now seized us and we are ready for the second scene, the visit, which will furnish us with the historical background of the case. A long scene, if measured by the clock, but psychologically very vivid, especially in the outbursts of sincerity and irony of Matilde Spina and her lover Belcredi, it successfully conveys the complexity and human depth of the main character, and increases our desire to see him in person. This wish is satisfied in the third scene, which also is long only if measured by the clock, but is extremely intense emotionally, and develops a dramatic tension that seems on the verge of exploding at any time, a tension prepared by the preceding scenes and now greatly increased by the behaviour of the hero, who keeps everybody holding their breath as if an explosion were actually expected.

The second act also begins in a relaxed mood: the visitors are discussing their impressions of the meeting with the 'madman.' Tension starts mounting again when Matilde begins to insist that she has been recognized; there is talk of a plan for a decisive encounter, and Frida, who is to play an important part in it, appears dressed as the Marchioness of Tuscany, very nervous and full of fears about her role; the expert, Landolfo, reveals a fixation of the 'madman': that Henry IV in the days of Canossa cherished a secret love for the Marchioness, his archenemy's hostess. Thus, the tension is high when in the following scene the visitors come before the 'madman' again to pretend to take leave of him. From him we know we can expect anything, that he will keep everyone in suspense, breathless, as in the first act, with that command of the situation that he enjoys, and which has become his macabre revenge. And this he does, tyrannizing over everybody. We wait for the rage to explode at any moment. Informed by Landolfo of his fixation, we hear a threatening ring in any allusion he makes to Matilde's daughter, who should be his wife since Matilde is dressed as his mother-in-law. We feel the tension mount, up to the final scene when Henry IV reveals his sanity to his councillors and valets. Then all terror leaves the stage in spite of Henry's attempt to maintain it by threatening to continue to be as tyrannical with the visitors, and if necessary with the attendants, as he has been up to now. We are no more convinced by his threats than are the councillors, who, in fact, offstage, during the first scene of the third act, inform the visitors of Henry's regained sanity.

Thus, at the beginning of the third act, the tension that would otherwise pervade the scene, with the two live portraits and Frida's visible fear, does not affect us greatly. Only after the first scene does the atmosphere again become charged. Henry IV admits that he is cured, becomes threatening, and warns Belcredi at once: 'Yes, recovered! I've really recovered! Ah, but not to put an end to it at once, as you would like to think!' (I 364). Sane now, that is, he starts playing Henry IV as before, tyrannizing, vomiting accusations against his visitors, particularly Belcredi. He is no longer insane, yet he is working himself up, and thus might at any time take for himself that just revenge which everyone feared he might take when he was mad; he is getting ready to strike by increasing the inner pressure, and the explosion finally comes when he sees that any desired understanding is impossible, that an attempt is being made to keep him in the position of perpetrator of the original joke rather than its victim. Blinded by rage, he loses control and commits an act of summary justice, after which he will have once again to make a choice: probably he will choose to take refuge again in the assumed madness and remain in the world of isolation that is by now familiar to him.

This rhythmic progression from minimal to maximal tension within each act is very frequent in Pirandello. And it effects a similar progression in the play as a whole, so that the opening is always calm and light, and the last scene the most dramatically tense. This element contributes greatly to an expressive unity, the very opposite of the 'erratic' quality we have seen attributed to *Henry IV*. Through this unifying element all the action and thematic developments converge on the non-cathartic conclusion of the play and find their ultimate meaning there.

6 *Each in His Own Way*: Mutability and Permanence in Life and Art

> We've got mere specks of certainty about ourselves and each other today,
> and they're different from yesterday's as they are from tomorrow's.
>
> (*Each in His Own Way*, I 172)

Each in His Own Way, the second play of the 'theatre trilogy,' returns to
and develops further some of the themes, situations, and innovative
theatrical techniques first brought into play in *Six Characters*; it is at
least equal in importance to the earlier work in the revolution Pirandello effected in the theatre of our time.

In *Six Characters* the family melodrama served as an occasion for quite
another drama, the drama of characters in search of their author, which
is to say, of definitive artistic form, the most powerful form of communication, without which their life is impossible. In *Each in His Own Way*,
Pirandello creates a supposedly 'real life' event reported in the daily
press, the suicide of the sculptor Giacomo La Vela following the discovery of an affair between his fiancée, Amelia Moreno, and Baron Nuti, his
sister's fiancé; the playwright translates this event for the stage into the
Giorgio Salvi–Delia Morello–Michele Rocca affair. Although it is not
rejected, like the family melodrama of *Six Characters*, as a sentimental,
late-nineteenth-century bourgeois situation, the 'real life' event functions similarly as the occasion for a deeper drama, one that focuses on
the theme of 'the continual reversals of our convictions and feelings' (I
158), the uncertainty and instability of our vision of ourselves and of the
world around us. And while the six characters were unable to leave the
stage in spite of their loud protestations, constrained to act their parts
when their drama was to be played out, here the stage couple and the

'real' one, while denigrating and abhorring each other when not face to face, must embrace and depart together, to everyone's dismay, when they meet and the return of the 'eternal moment' (I 99) compels them to act out their destined roles.

Each in His Own Way also develops the Pirandellian chorus character further. He has appeared in the Laudisi of *Right You Are, if You Think You Are*, as the author's version of the *raisonneur* of the grottesco theatre, usually somewhat detached from the central event of the drama, who observes it from a certain distance and comments on its meaning, acting as the author's mouthpiece. In *Six Characters* he split into at least two characters who were at the centre of the dramatic event, those characters who were most conscious of their nature *as* characters and therefore most able to intelligently examine the themes of the play. Here (although he will later split into the many commentators of the 'intermezzi') he reappears as a single character, Diego Cinci, who, unlike the imperturbable Laudisi, is immersed in the dramatic event and lives it as passionately as all the others, a victim himself of the contradictions he illustrates, so that he too will fall by the way with the others. But differently from the others he is able to 'see himself living,' as he sees the others, and is capable of explaining himself to himself and the others to themselves, revealing their hidden motives, acting as their conscience; hence the irony of his speeches (from the early dialogues of the first act to his last comments at the conclusion of the second) evolves into a pure instance of Pirandellian *umorismo*.

In *Six Characters* a number of parallels express the dichotomy between artistic creation and its actual communication: the characters of the family melodrama and those of the real drama of the characters in search of their author; the Pirandellian characters and the actor-characters who are to perform the family melodrama and who for the Pirandellian characters represent the public, the audience. In *Each in His Own Way* the parallels are multiplied. Being a *comédie à clef*, it has in the background the 'persons' of the La Vela–Moreno–Nuti affair and the characters-as-persons Moreno and Nuti of the 'intermezzi,' acted out by the actors who play *their* roles (of these the leading actress in her role as an actress and not in her role as a character, yet *because* she has played the character, is slapped in the face by the character-as-person Moreno). There are also the spectator-characters who during the 'intermezzi' criticize the quality of the play and the acting, discuss and pass judgment on the characters, or, as Diego Cinci does, on the logic, or lack of it, of the dramatic event that has taken place, and is taking place, before their eyes.

While the six characters have no counterparts in everyday reality, since they are exclusively 'characters,' inventions of the author's imagination, here even the persons of everyday life (La Vela–Moreno–Nuti) have been invented; the characters of the dramatic event (Salvi–Morello–Rocca) are supposed to be the dramatic rendering of the former, except that even the persons of 'real life' are later translated into the characters-as-persons of the 'intermezzi' (Moreno–Nuti), who have seen themselves played by the actors of the theatrical company in the characters of the *comédie à clef* and are horrified (as the six characters, seeing themselves played by the theatrical company, were horrified by the poverty of the interpretation they had witnessed). Their distress appears to be caused by their impression that the mirror of the play 'not only freezes [them] with their own image, but sends it back to [them] with a grimace that's an unrecognizable distortion of [them]selves' (as the Son in *Six Characters* had complained and as Eugenio Levi[1] mistakenly thinks is the case here). But later it becomes clear that this was a wrong impression, and that if anything this time the mirror has sent back an all-too-true image; their revulsion is thus not the disgust of the six characters before the distortion, but the revulsion that comes with the discovery of an appalling truth ('*An intelligent spectator*: No, no, gentlemen. That was the most natural thing! They saw themselves as if in a mirror and they objected violently, especially to that last gesture of theirs!' I 197). Pirandello elsewhere describes such a revelation as a moment when 'our soul sheds all its customary pretences and our eyes become sharper and penetrating; ... we see ourselves living' and 'are seized by a strange feeling, as if in a flash a reality quite different from the one we usually perceive were revealed to us.'[2]

If the family melodrama of *Six Characters* cannot be performed because there is no script, and if the script does not exist because the sentimental bourgeois drama of the six failed to interest Pirandello except as an occasion for another play, and if they succeed as characters because they 'live the drama' of a rejection they cannot accept, the characters of *Each in His Own Way* succeed because they live a drama of incompleteness, a drama that goes on without end in everyone's life – the drama of insecurity, inconsistency, uncertainty, of doubt about oneself and others, a continuing shifting of convictions.

If the six characters live the endless contradiction of willing and not willing, accepting and rejecting their painful dramatic roles, seeking the definitive artistic form with which they will later be dissatisfied, but which they cannot do without if they want to communicate, to live,

Delia Morello and Michele Rocca live the contradiction of attraction and rejection, a tragic condition of willing and not willing, believing and disbelieving ('They say one thing, and then they say the opposite!' I 158), a condition shared by all the characters of the play, whether they are conscious of it like Diego Cinci or unaware like his friends.

As in *Six Characters* 'everyone ... believes he is "one"' while 'he is instead "many"' ... in accord with all the possibilities of being that are in us' (I 72), so also in *Each in His Own Way* every character believes that he or she is 'one' while in reality they are 'many,' different in the eyes of those who see and judge them and constantly changing in their own eyes; because in everyone, 'humoristically,' a character and its opposite, and many intermediate characters, exist simultaneously. Thus, the protagonists of the first act, Doro and Francesco, according to Diego Cinci's diagnosis, have both fallen victim, albeit unawares, to the fascination of the femme fatale and are equally infatuated with Miss Morello. But at a party the previous night Francesco has denounced her with some passion, repeating publicly what is usually whispered in private about her, while Doro has no less passionately defended her. Their differing behaviour was due to the fact that Francesco is the older and less spontaneous and has made use, before revealing himself to the public, of those weapons of intellectual and self-ironic defence that Belcredi tells us Henry IV used before becoming insane, when he discovered that he had abandoned himself to one of his spontaneous sentimental effusions ('He'd right away, at the very moment he was feverish with enthusiasm' and 'sometimes he'd explode in really comical fits of anger against himself,' I 313). The more spontaneous Doro, by contrast, tries to use them after having revealed himself. Francesco, by accusing her in public, has subconsciously sought to convince himself and his acquaintances that he is not infatuated with Miss Morello. Doro tries to do the same by switching to Francesco's side and adopting his arguments, but only when it is too late, after reflection – when, that is, Francesco, having reflected himself, has realized the unfairness of his action and is ready to admit that Doro was right. While Francesco does it calmly, however, since it is safe for him to do so, Doro experiences one of those 'fits of anger' that seized Henry IV when he realized he had incautiously revealed his sentimental impulses, and the victim of that anger is Francesco, who with his accusations has provoked Doro into revealing his infatuation ('And now he has the gall to come here and tell me that *I* was right! ... After he made me everybody's laughingstock last night, the object of all kinds of nasty ideas ... urging me on, compromising me, getting me to say things that had never crossed my mind!' I 142). Hence, before Francesco who has changed his mind, Doro retreats to the position he held the previous night and calls Francesco a *'pulcinella,'* not realizing that if Francesco is a weathercock he is one too, having changed his mind twice. Or it may be because he is aware of this that he retreats (prompted as well, perhaps, by the mild irony with which Cinci has greeted his intended retraction, as an attempt to deny his infatuation) and stands fast on his original position, which moments later Miss Morello herself will show him is no more firmly grounded than that of Francesco.

Doro's position is in fact demolished during a dialogue with Miss Morello, who has come to thank him for the defence he had mounted the night before with arguments and ideas that have revealed her to herself, allowed her to see herself as she never did before. In their lively exchange she repeats his words with approval, completes the sentences he starts, as he completes hers; their agreement is total and enthusiastic. But when the dialogue moves on to the enumeration of Francesco's accusations, she comes to see them, after her initial disbelief, as equally illuminating, allowing her to see herself as she never has before, and ends by suggesting that perhaps Francesco has read her with equal clarity, that she might very well be the woman he accused her of being. Because in Delia there still coexist the adolescent Lilí who learned to somersault from the gypsies and the mature femme fatale whose lovers are ready to leap to their death for her; the Morello who 'generously' eloped with Rocca to save the young artist Salvi from a misguided marriage to her and the 'proud' Morello who eloped with Rocca, the prime obstacle to her being introduced to the Salvi household, to show the Salvis what a low hypocrite their terribly 'respectable' future son-in-law actually was; and the Morello who eloped with Rocca because she was fatally attracted to him. Like Miss Moreno, whose experience she portrays, 'everybody knows who she is' (I 123), but actually all only 'think' they know who she really is.

She is, in fact, a development of the character of Mrs Ponza, who throughout *Right You Are* is presented to us by other people's opinions of her – her husband's, her mother's, her neighbours' (so that at the end of the play when she is asked in person she is compelled to say that for herself she is nothing, she is only who she is believed to be). Miss Morello, having first been presented by other people's opinions, comes on the scene herself in search of her own identity, which she has not yet been able to grasp, her view of herself still in flux like the others' and shifting now towards one, now towards another of the opinions others express about her: the innocent Morello in the bosom of her family during her adolescence, the honest, sincere Morello seen by Doro, the vindictive Morello projected by Francesco, the sadomasochist who embraces Michele Rocca in the end.

Michele similarly, of course, can be seen as the model fiancé of Salvi's little sister, the seducer of Miss Morello who elopes with her to save Salvi from a disastrous marriage, and the sadomasochist who is fatally attracted to Miss Morello. The first-act dialogue between Doro and Delia, in which she first agrees with Doro's opinions and then disconcerts him by agreeing with Francesco's, is paralleled by the dialogue in the second act between Rocca and Francesco in which Rocca goes far beyond agreement with Francesco's accusations against Miss Morello, stating that she did not seduce him but was seduced by him in an attempt to show Salvi her unworthiness as he had bet he could. But when he and Delia meet face to face all their declared reasons crumble as it becomes clear that they eloped because of a reciprocal attraction stronger than the repulsion they must have felt at the thought of the mortal blow they were about to inflict upon the Salvis – an attraction that must be even stronger now that Salvi has killed himself, and which even in the end they refuse to confess to, evasively invoking some fatal bond of spilled blood that now ties them together forever.

One of the major themes of this drama is in fact that of appearance and reality, already developed in *Right You Are* and *Six Characters*, of the subjectivity of our perceptions and beliefs, and hence of our need to find them corroborated by others. A sub-theme that flows from this, and is more strongly dramatized in the present work, is that of uncertainty, doubt, contradiction, which, as we have seen, dominates the life of all its characters. A new theme is developed here as well, introduced but not fully explored in *Six Characters*: the relationship between the truth of artistic reality and that of real life.

As in the preceding works, Pirandello successfully avoids intellectualization, abstract discussion, and lengthy argumentation, always fatal to poetry and drama. He expresses the human problem of the subjectivity of perception and the difficulty of communication, of the mutability of our convictions, in an intensely vivid and innovative theatre, in dramatic action that is always novel and unpredictable, engaging in its fictitious imitation of the 'real life' of the daily papers, so fully integrated that even the 'chorus,' Diego Cinci, is totally drawn into it. It is through dramatic action that the relationship between the truth of artistic reality and that of real life is explored, especially in the extraordinary 'inter-mezzi' in which the characters of the event from 'real life' encounter both the characters of the play based on it and the actors who portray them, when the lobby becomes the stage on which the characters of art can meet those of life. A superbly original theatrical imagination has put the relation between art and life on stage, before our astonished eyes.

However much it owes to its theatrical originality, the drama and the poetic unity of this work are grounded firmly in its central human pre-dicament: every character is caught up in the same fundamental con-flict – 'the drama in which and thanks to which he is a character,' as Pirandello would say (I 40) – between uncertainty about oneself and others, about the reality in which one moves, and the intense although unconscious need to be anchored in some certainty, to be delivered into the arms of a destiny that will calm all anxiety, to find a form for one's being and behaviour – a universal human need dramatized in *Six Char-acters* and *Henry IV*. The form that Henry IV borrows from history as a means of avoiding the minefield of an unpredictable and uncontrolla-ble present, the 'real life' characters, Moreno and Nuti, in this play, borrow from the suggestions of a work of art. In Pirandello's view life is an 'incessant fluctuation between contradictory terms, an oscillation between opposite poles';[3] clearly in this drama he once again places his characters between two opposite necessities, two contrasting but unde-niable realities of daily life, and this shared inner drama of all the char-acters gives a sense of necessity and precision, of perfect economy, to every event, speech, and gesture of the play, and a strong poetic unity to the whole.

This unity and dramatic economy are already at work in the first scenes, which immediately establish and dramatize the atmosphere of uncertainty, doubt, and shifting convictions on the one hand, and an anxious need for certainty and stability on the other – the atmosphere of conflict that will engulf all the characters up to the last verbal exchange of the play. The first act opens with three dialogues. A young man and an old man speak:

Thin young man: But what's *your* opinion?
Old friend of the family: My opinion? I don't know! What do the others think?
Young man: Well – some one thing, some another.
Old friend: Of course, of course! Everyone has their own opinion.

Young man: But, to tell the truth, nobody seems to stick to it very firmly, since everybody, like you, wants to know what the others think before they say anything.
Old friend: I stick to mine all right ...
Young man: Because, judging from what you're saying, nobody can have firm opinions!
Old friend: And don't you think that that's already having an opinion? (I 127–8)

Two young ladies exchange confidences:

The first: You are giving me a whole new lease on life! Tell me more, more!
The second: But, look, it's nothing more than my personal impression! ...
The first: In the meantime I don't know if I'm doing the right thing or not ... And how do I feel? I swear I don't know any more! Everything's shifting, changing, insubstantial. I turn this way, that way, I laugh, I go into a corner to cry. Always restless! In anguish! Constantly hiding from myself, ashamed of seeing myself changing every minute! (I 128–9)

Then to a group of friends Diego Cinci asserts the impossibility of maintaining certitudes, the shifting of our beliefs as we encounter different ideas and circumstances, the fact that even conscience, that stable point of reference, is only 'the others inside you' (I 130), that the mutable opinions of others determine our actions. The act then moves through a series of dialogues in which the shifting of convictions is dramatized, including the clash between Doro and Francesco, who have both embraced beliefs opposite to the ones put forward in their debate the previous night, but now draw back to their original positions and challenge each other to a duel no longer exclusively verbal. The act culminates in the crucial dialogue between Doro and Miss Morello in which the platform on which the paladin has taken his stand gives way, and with the woman's departure no one knows any more to what certitude he can cling: Doro and all his family and friends are shaken, they no longer know why there is going to be a duel, perhaps a fatal one, and, except for Diego and Francesco, all disappear from the play after the first-act curtain, having lived this radical and deeply disquieting drama of the constant shifting of certitudes.

The entire work develops through repeated clashes of characters and ideas, including the final encounter of Morello and Rocca and the verbal battles of the 'intermezzi,' and through the continual shifting of the characters' beliefs, in dialogue that beautifully combines a strong sense of verbal economy and vivid concision with the sense of uncertainty and indecision of people who are both trapped in the jaws of doubt and fighting to escape it ('And don't you think that that's already having an opinion? – Yes, but a negative one! – Better than nothing, eh? better than nothing!' I 128; 'No, no! read, read yourself clearly!' I 140; 'The fact is that I have recognized myself, "recognized," understand?, in everything you said about me,' I 144). And so the intensity of the drama does not flag even when questions of philosophy or aesthetics are discussed or simply alluded to ('Your conscience actually means "the others inside you,"' I 130; 'But is it legitimate to take the subject of a work of art from life?' I 162).

Every character who becomes involved in the action of this drama is caught up in the universal conflict, so that not only can the others not formulate a firm opinion of him or her, but they themselves are never sure of their own convictions, of their own reality; all are cruelly driven to a constant alteration of their ideas, to the repeated revelation of themselves in a new light when they thought they had finally succeeded in expressing themselves and being perceived with a certain finality. All are doomed to perceive and experience themselves 'in their own way,' including the protagonists of the lively exchanges in the lobby, which give the concluding scenes (and with them the whole play) an extraordinary dramatic charge:

> *The favourably inclined spectators*: Ah! Here we are! / All set! / It's going really well, isn't it? / Ah! fresh air at last! / That last scene with the woman! / And she, the woman! / And the scene with those two switching from one side to the other!
> *The spectators who are not favourably inclined (at the same time)*: The usual word games! Go figure what they mean! / They're pulling our legs! / It seems to me he's beginning to feel a bit overconfident! / I didn't understand a thing! / A bunch of riddles! / Heck, if the theatre has to be torture!
> *One of the not favourably inclined spectators to the other group*: Oh, you understand everything, don't you?
> *Another not favourably inclined one*: Of course, of course! All geniuses, those guys!
> *One of the favourably inclined group (approaching)*: Are you talking to me?
> *The first of the not favourably inclined group*: Not to you, to him! *(Pointing to another of the favourably inclined spectators).*
> *The one who has been pointed at (approaching)*: To me? Are you talking to me?

The first of the not favourably inclined group: To you, to you! You wouldn't understand even a school play! (I 157–8)

In this obsessive nightmare nobody understands or agrees with or influences anyone else, to the ironic point that when one person *has* changed ideas and is ready to agree with another, the latter has moved to the opinions of the former and the two are ready to start battling again with real weapons. Each character emerges from one illusion and enters another, in a state of constant uncertainty and instability. Every moment of the play is sustained by a dramatic tension that is rarely present in the plays of philosophical or political debate that have become popular in recent decades (although the genre is hardly new, harking back to G.B. Shaw's 'discussion plays' of the beginning of the century).

The dramatic intensity of the play is also enhanced by Pirandello's original handling of the complexity of the various levels of the drama: the 'actual' event is translated into a theatrical event seen and judged both by the characters of the 'actual' event and the spectators of the theatrical event; the instability of human psychology is dramatized in the protagonists of the actual event (Moreno–Nuti), in the protagonists of the theatrical translation (Morello–Rocca), in those who discuss the actual event (Doro–Francesco–Diego, etc.), in those who discuss its theatrical translation (the spectators, including Moreno and Nuti). The dramatic intensity of the play strengthens its perceptions: that art understands the persons of real life better than they can understand themselves; that art penetrates to the depths of their souls and 'foresees' what they will do 'before our very eyes against their will' (I 197); that art reveals the truth in an ever-changing, illusory world; that only art achieves that form which life – which is chaotic, shifting, inchoate – yearns for; that art is a mirror for life rather than a mirror of life.

In fact, as the play develops, the relationship between art and life emerges as its central theme. While illusion and subjectivity are explored mainly in the first two acts and their 'intermezzo,' the theme that rises to final importance remains somewhat hidden, although always implicit, assuming a primary position in the second part and dominating the last 'intermezzo,' a masterful Pirandellian explosion of action and dialogue:

Voices of the crowd of spectators: Miss Moreno! Miss Moreno! / Who is Miss Moreno? / They've slapped the leading lady in the face! / Who? Who

slapped who in the face? / Miss Moreno! Miss Moreno! / And who's Miss
Moreno? / The leading lady? / No, no, they've slapped the author in the
face! / The author? Slapped in the face? / Who? Who slapped who? / Miss
Moreno! No, the leading lady! / The author's slapped the leading lady? /
No, no, the other way around! / The leading lady slapped the author in the
face! / No, certainly not! Miss Moreno's slapped the leading lady! (I 93)

Miss Moreno: My own voice! My exact gestures! All my mannerisms ...
What nerve! Me, me, embracing that man!? ...
Spectators' voices: Look, look! / There they are, over there! ... / They're
playing the scene! ...
The intelligent spectator: Right, exactly so! They did, as they had to, before
our eyes, against their will, what art had foreseen! (I 196–7)

In the last 'choral intermezzo' the relationship between art and life is
effectively dramatized by bringing together and mixing art and life,
getting the 'audience' to take part in the action on the stage, abolishing
the separation through noisy, action-filled scenes rather than abstract
discussion.

The entire play develops with rigorous dramatic economy. Not a
scene, not a sentence, is superfluous, although the dramatization of the
themes of uncertainty, of the subjectivity and instability of opinions,
might suggest that the dramatic action itself undergoes turnabouts and
sudden halts. The action of the characters at the Palegaris' at the end of
the first act, and at the Savios' at the end of the second, has exhausted
its charge and its function; the characters are engulfed in uncertainty
and their role *as* active characters is liquidated, after they witness in disbelief the capsizing of all their expectations and the raw reality of the
final embrace, and the play as the dramatization of these first themes is
completed. From this perspective it could be considered a two-act play,
and Pirandello humorously gives us the option of viewing it as a play
in two or three acts (I 122).

It unquestionably is, however, a three-act play – the third act being
the last 'intermezzo' – as a dramatization of the theme of the relationship between artistic truth and the truth of real life, a theme repeatedly
hinted at from the initial stage directions, and which becomes increasingly clear until in the final 'intermezzo' it emerges as the primary and
conclusive theme of the play. And from this point of view the structure
of the play neither breaks down nor remains open to infinity, with the

falling of the conscious and unconscious support of the convictions and conventions of the various characters, but continues to hold and develop to its conclusion, with the dramatic concision of the great masterpieces, in which nothing is superfluous and a poetic logic controls every detail. All the action that develops the earlier themes, and which in this sense could be considered concluded with the end of the second act, with the embrace of Morello and Rocca under the horrified eyes of Francesco and his guests, is also functional to the development of the major theme carried by the four primary characters, Morello–Rocca–Moreno–Nuti, both in their clashes with the observing characters whom they destroy by the end of each of the two acts, and in their own stormy and conclusive encounters. The four protagonists of the bloody event must first live the drama of uncertainty, doubt, and instability with the secondary characters. Like the latter they experience the illusion of finding the explanation of their own actions and motivations; in the latter they think they have found their defenders and paladins, or their enemies and denigrators – only to come to understand at last the falseness of their entire interpretation, and the fatal reciprocal repulsion and attraction that constitutes their ultimate fate.

Both protagonists and non-protagonists must first live the drama of shifting beliefs that drives them to the edge of madness between a truth just found and the next one. And the brilliant actor who has played the part of Diego Cinci warns at the end that it is a permanent condition which is going to repeat itself forever; that once outside the door of the theatre lobby, god knows how many more discoveries those two had still to make; that their embrace was not the last discovery of a revolting though undeniable truth; that, in sum, if there had been a third act, a sequel of surprising new discoveries would have occurred (I 197–8). Therefore, the play might well stop at the end of the second act, if the eternal proposal of the unforeseeable were its only concern.

Once the dramatic experience of the uncertainty and instability of convictions has been lived through and exhausted – a condition that is permanent, an experience that is repetitive, and which in the play can therefore be interrupted at any point – then the play can bring to the fore the theme of the relationship between art and life, and carry this theme to its dramatic conclusion in the last 'intermezzo,' intermingling the characters of the world of art and those of daily reality, abolishing the separation between art and life the better to dramatize their difference.

Each in His Own Way represents a further development of the themes, situations, and innovative theatrical techniques first brought into play in *Six Characters*, here even more daringly innovative in the use of theatrical language and of the stage space, and in the translation into drama of the metatheatrical themes.

7 Opposing Aims of the Artist's Vocation in *The Mountain Giants*

Yes, the work is alive in me, but that's not enough! It must live among men!

(*The Mountain Giants*, II 1346)

Like *Six Characters, Each in His Own Way,* and Pirandello's last major work, *The Mountain Giants, Tonight We Improvise* deals with the problem of art, and of the theatre in particular, dramatizing the problem of the authorship of a dramatic work. A theatrical company rebels against the overwhelming domination of its director, refusing to be 'puppets in his hands' (I 215). They complain that his intrusions and impositions act as a sudden, unexpected cold shower on the warmth of their acting whenever they succeed in entering their character and in living and suffering his or her passions the way the character feels and wants to live them. The director pretends to allow them the independence they seek, and they are lulled into believing that they are really the creators of the play they are putting together, following the plot line of a Pirandellian short story (once again the staging of a bourgeois melodrama functions as a pretext for the real Pirandellian drama about the contested authorship of a theatrical work). But in the end the actors are no longer sure they were the creators and suspect that the director has actually controlled them from beginning to end, despite their apparent victory in the vociferous scene in which they sidelined him.

Just as the independence the actors claim is shown to be fictitious, or at least unproductive, so, inevitably, the vaunted independence of the director from the author must be considered fictitious and unproductive. The director appropriates some ideas expressed by Pirandello in earlier works: for instance, that 'a writer's work ends the moment he sets down the last word.' But then he adds on his own that this finished work then belongs to 'the reading public and the literary critics' and not yet to 'the theatre audience and the drama critics'; that 'in the theatre the writer's work no longer exists' (I 208), and we have only the 'stage creation' the director makes of it, which is 'his alone,' since it is he who interprets the play, chooses the actors and assigns their parts, decides what the designers, stage managers, and electricians must do (I 209). He appropriates the Pirandellian idea that 'a work of art is fixed forever in an immutable form which represents the poet's liberation from his creative labour, the perfect calm reached after the turbulence of that labour' in order to authorize his own conclusion that 'where nothing moves any more, where everything rests in perfect calm,' there 'can no longer be any life' (I 209), for 'liberation and calm can be achieved only when life ends'; that, consequently, 'if a work of art lives again it is only because' the director is able 'to set it free from the fixity of its form, to rouse this form ... into vital movement,' and 'it is [he] then who gives it life' (I 210).

It is important to remember that these are not Pirandello's theories[1] (some of today's directors seem to believe they have Pirandello's approval for their freewheeling treatment of even the most hallowed classics, including Pirandello's), but those of his deluded director-character, a rather comical, dwarfish creature ('a pipsqueak of a man not much taller than an arm's length, but who makes up for it with an enormous head of hair,' I 206), a self-important, pompous, petulant figure, ridiculously named Dr Hinkfuss. They are no less illusory than the actors' illusory independence from their director. It is clear in fact from the very first scene that the performance would degenerate into irremediable chaos if the director were not there to give it a certain degree of logical direction, and that this direction, what there is of it, actually comes from the author's script from which the director never departs mentally, just as, physically, he keeps it tightly tucked under his arm at all times. However, as in *Six Characters*, the melodrama to be staged remains fragmentary, full of 'stumbling blocks' and setbacks, so much so that Hinkfuss finds it necessary to apologize for it to the audience and promise a smoother performance for the following night, while the leading actor shouts that the chaos is all due to the director's ambition to take the author's place ('We must have the author!' I 289). No chaos, however, mars the real, 'Pirandellian' play, which is not the pretextual drama of jealousy, but centres on the problem of authorship in an art form like drama, whose realization of course requires the collaboration of stage designers, actors, and directors, but whose essential life comes from the vital charge that the author has given that 'frozen' life in the written work. The definitive artistic form seals and protects the work against the infinite potential for inaccurate interpretation by the many Hinkfusses who will get their hands on it in the future.

This is clearly a complex work, with many different dramatic levels and the many levels of meaning and expression characteristic of the most clever metatheatre of our time, and for this reason perhaps a rather difficult play to interpret and to stage, requiring of directors, actors, designers, and choreographers a clear grasp of the real themes of the text and considerable skill in realizing them dramatically. As in the other two plays on the art of the theatre, the actors must be able to act out the 'Pirandellian' drama at the same time as they are performing the melodrama. But in *Six Characters* and *Each in His Own Way* the metatheatrical themes (artistic communication, the power and elusiveness of definitive artistic form, the authorship and inviolability of the dramatic text) were intertwined with painful and compelling existential themes (the difficulty of human communication, given the relativism of human perception, the subjectivity of all forms of communication, the mutability of the reality that is the object of human communication, etc.), while in the present play, these metatheatrical themes virtually dominate the work from the first verbal exchanges to the end. Thus, perhaps more than the earlier masterpieces, *Tonight We Improvise* requires an exceptionally subtle and skilful production to bring out its cogency and power (which has rarely been the case on the infrequent occasions when it has been performed).

A fourth play dealing with the problems of artistic creativity and communication is the one Pirandello was trying to finish when he died, *The Mountain Giants*. It belongs to a group of plays written during the last years of his life that he called 'myths' rather than 'comedies' (the latter being the term he employed, following the usage of the time, for most of his plays, whether they contained comic elements or were utterly serious). 'Myths' is used probably to suggest that they pose only remote, utopian, improbable solutions to the perennial and compelling human problems they dramatize. (The word in Italian can in fact mean something fantastic and visionary.)

The first of these plays, *The New Colony*, explores the possibilities of a socio-political solution of a democratic nature to the old evils of poverty and social neglect: hunger, unemployment, prostitution, the political and economic oppression of the underclass of the slums of a seaport city. A group of these people decide to start a new life on a small, sunny, edenic island, once used as a penal colony but abandoned because it is in danger of being sunk by the earthquakes frequent in the region. This will actually happen at the conclusion of the play. However, before Nature moves to put its seal on the new socio-political experiment, adversarial forces both internal and external have intervened to shipwreck it. Though initiated with the best of intentions and based on the principles of the will of the majority and the good of the community, the experiment fails because it is opposed from within by the rancour, spite, and selfishness of the participants, and besieged from outside by larger interests that very successfully exploit the weaknesses and incite the selfish ambitions of the participants. The entire experiment had already crumbled by the time the island is finally submerged, leaving alone with her child on a crag above the waters the former prostitute, who during the life of the experiment had become an extraordinary example of moral regeneration and sincere altruism.

Many critics have concluded that by this miraculous survival of mother and son Pirandello meant that the solution is to be sought not so much in the adoption of more democratic social and political institutions, as in a return to primordial and instinctual feelings; in the 'instinctual regression of the subconscious visceral feelings,'[2] as Marziano Guglielminetti, for instance, puts it in an essay that sums up a long line of critical thinking. But this persistent misinterpretation is based on a reading of the new love that rules the behaviour of the former prostitute, La Spera (a name closely related to the word 'hope'), as exclusively 'maternal love' ('the exaltation of maternal love as the primary source of social redemption,' Guglielminetti adds, p. 246), while Pirandello dramatizes, and in the end has La Spera define, her feelings in communal and indeed universal terms: 'Here I made myself a new person, God, in your presence, in the light of your sun, I alone filled with *love for all!*' (II 1153 [my emphasis]; Guglielminetti's misreading is particularly unfortunate coming as it does as his commentary on this statement, which he considers a crucial passage in the play, p. 246).[3]

In another serious misinterpretation, Guglielminetti follows several other critics in finding a parallel between La Spera and the *meretrix magna* of the Apocalypse, and in establishing an identification with the psychoanalytical archetype 'of the Great Earth Mother, who generates and devours her own children,' and who prevents her sons 'from detaching themselves from her, from developing their own autonomous identity.'[4] One need only consider briefly what sort of 'autonomous identity' this bastard son of the *meretrix magna* would have 'developed' in the hands of the opportunist Currao and the gang of the 'big boss,' Padron Nocio, who tried hard to take the child away from her.

Such misreadings of Pirandello's 'myths' resulted in the attribution to their author of a number of absurd theses. We are assured, for example, that *'The New Colony*, as a "social myth," proposes, as the only possible form of rebellion against the bourgeois world, the regression of the individual to the womb, which demonstrates that the detachment of the son from the mother is impossible – a thesis amply documented throughout the literature of the *"belle époque,"* and not only in its theatre' (p. 248). It is absurd to propose that Pirandello, who from his earliest stories to his last plays dramatized countless possible forms of rebellion against the bourgeois world, would have considered 'the regression of the individual to the womb' the *only* form of rebellion; absurd that in 1928 Pirandello would regress to a theory 'amply documented' more than a quarter of a century earlier in the literature of the *belle époque*, that is, in a literature and a theatre whose premises he had dedicated the work of a lifetime to proving false; absurd to propose that Pirandello, whose 'myths' explore and dramatize possible new forms of regeneration and renewal, would call for a 'regression that paralyses any possibility of renewal' (p. 248); absurd because Pirandello's resolution, which is clearly symbolic, not realistic, dramatizes the fact that only La Spera and her son among the participants in the experiment deserve to be saved, and that the presence of one just person is not enough to save a community (as Lot's family was not enough to save Sodom and Gomorrah). The final cry of La Spera – 'Oh God, I'm here alone with you, my son, above the waters!' (II 1158) – does not express the victory of the Great Earth Mother who devours her own children; it more likely suggests that the 'renewal' might be brought about not only by those who are capable of regeneration in that 'love for all men,' but also by those who will be schooled from infancy in that universal love ('It'll be my duty to teach him what he needs to know ... before others bite him with their venom ... I'll have the time and I'll find the way to make him wise and good,' II 1126).

For if it is clear that the experiment in democratic socio-political renewal is a failure, it is equally clear that the selflessness, generosity, and love that inspire the behaviour of the woman are the only force, new or old, that might effect a general renewal, as it has effected an individual one. But La Spera in the end is disastrously alone in experiencing these emotions; the forces of ambition, greed, and selfishness are just as ancient and deeply rooted, and her enlightened and generous behaviour is overwhelmed by the ignorant and selfish behaviour of the others, including even the best intentioned among them. It is not so much the programmatic adoption of a new political system or a new social order that is needed, according to the Pirandello of *The New Colony*, as a personal rebirth, an inner conversion to selflessness of the individual soul. Good government and social justice will be its natural outcome.

Thus, in the next 'myth,' *Lazarus*, the solution to the evils of the world explored by Pirandello is a religious conversion to the principle of love. If in *The New Colony* the attempt to implement a more just political and social vision had failed because the hearts of the participants had not been renewed and the old selfishness had strangled the new intentions, the road to the resurrection of the old man, the dead and already decaying Lazarus, must be the conversion to the commandment of love and the renunciation of individual egoism.

Three different religious attitudes are contrasted in *Lazarus*. One is rigid, stern, inquisitional, embodied by the head of the family, Diego Spina. It imposes renunciation and suffering as the unavoidable price in this life for the reward of the next life, which is the real one. This vision obviously offers neither redemption nor regeneration for suffering humanity in this world; and when faith in the reality of the afterlife is seriously undermined, self-denying asceticism is replaced by an unbridled and selfish pursuit of pleasure, as happens to Diego Spina himself. A different religious attitude is embraced by Diego's wife, Sarah, who, when her husband's rigidity has desiccated family life and driven his son to spiritual and his daughter to physical paralysis, leaves him for a simple, honest peasant, with whom she has two healthy children. She believes that the kingdom of God is to be created and enjoyed in this life first of all, in a healthy immersion in the life of Nature, in daily work, in the enjoyment of one's exertion, of the fruits of the earth and its pleasures. A third attitude, one Pirandello would like to believe leads to true regeneration (Silvio D'Amico, in his *Storia del teatro drammatico*, speaks convincingly – not 'thoughtlessly,' as Guglielminetti says [p. 233] – of a 'will to believe' in these last plays, that is, a quest for a faith acceptable to his intellectual and rationalistic bent),[5] centres on a return to the simple tenets of the Gospel within a neo-idealistic intellectual framework. Diego's son Lucio had been urged by his father to become a priest. While pursuing a doctorate at the university after his ordination, he overcomes a profound spiritual and intellectual crisis that threatens his vocation, through the discovery of the gospel of universal love. This love must be lived not for reward or punishment in another life (for the human body is mortal and the life of the individual ends with death), but because the spirit of the individual is a spark of the great fire, of the eternal Universal Spirit, embodied in the individual and returned to eternity after his death. The essence of this great fire is love, and the individual who owes his life to this love must live it. Lucio postulates this integration of the individual in the immortality of the Universal Spirit and the law of love that must rule the world on an intuition of a truth that seems to him irrefutable: those who have suffered undeservedly in this life must of necessity meet with a love in the next life that compensates for the injustice (God must 'restore wings to those who were deprived of feet to walk on this earth' [II 1216], he says, as his young sister sits paralysed before him); that love is the essence of the Spirit and the reason for its generating the individual. This intuition ('I feel that there is') becomes a postulate ('there must be, there must be!') and then a belief ('there is, there is!' II 1216), the centre of his new faith.

Thus, in these two 'myths' the passionate search for definitive certainties leads to truths that seem to lack the persuasiveness and universality of absolutes even for Pirandello himself, who also failed to create in them powerful, persuasive works of art. And ultimately the two plays seem to confirm the idea that, for their unending search for the roots of their suffering, the Pirandellian characters almost always derive more anguish than knowledge. This bleak outcome is the conclusion of the author's last unfinished play as well (the last of the 'myths,' which is, however, one of Pirandello's dramatic masterpieces), a final play on the nature of art as an expression of human creativity, of the highest, most divine of human activities, which is nevertheless probably destined to rejection or incomprehension.

The Mountain Giants explores the problems of art not exclusively in terms of its power and permanence as a means of communication, but as a way of life, a vocation, and perhaps even as a means of renewal and salvation (given the uncertain outcome of the quest for possible political or religious solutions). For, if the poet's vocation is of a communicative rather than a solipsistic nature, and he realizes it faithfully, communicating to his fellow man the truths which, though subjective, are the fruits of his passionate search, then he has fulfilled the task he was called to – he has made an important contribution to human life. This play confronts and dramatizes the entire 'body of problems of the theater,' the 'very life of the theater,' in the words of Strehler,[6] but its central concern is with the problem of the communicative ends of the theatre and of art in general. *The Mountain Giants* contrasts two ways of viewing the essence and the ends of art, in the familiar context of a clash between two ways of viewing reality and thereby shaping human behaviour, represented by the Pirandellian characters on the one hand and the self-righteous and philistine world of the bourgeoisie on the other.

The clash between the Pirandellian characters and the philistinism of the bourgeois world occurs in two separate phases. Before the action begins, the 'Scalognati' have long since radically rejected and abandoned an ungrateful and insensitive world and taken refuge in a solitary villa abandoned because it is supposedly haunted. The theatrical company that reaches the villa at the opening of the play, pulling a poor token of a 'Thespian' cart, has been dwindling in number, energy, and means through the frustration and suffering of two years of vain efforts to overcome public indifference and insensitivity to what they believe to be a splendid poetic script. They have come to the villa only by some chance misunderstanding; actually they are still searching for the audience the Scalognati have long abandoned, because they still passionately cherish the idea of the essentially communicative function of art, the idea that poetry 'must live among people' (II 1346). At the end of the play (in what should have been the fourth 'time frame,' which Pirandello was unable to complete before he died; a four-page outline was provided by his son Stefano on the basis of conversations with his father) the 'Thespians' and some of the Scalognati will again face the obtuseness and deafness of the outside world, with even worse consequences, since it will no longer be the world of the Victorian bourgeoisie but a world already in the process of rhinocerization, the era of industrial capitalism and of anonymous masses enslaved to consumerism. The Mountain Giants, engrossed in their 'enormous enterprises – excavations, foundations, reservoirs, factories, roads, farms' (II 1360) – even on the occasion of a marriage linking their powerful families, 'have no time for such things, so extensive and so many are the projects they must attend to' (II 1372), and display their magnanimity by allowing the Thespians to perform their play before 'their servants and the crews of workers they employ for their enormous projects' (II 1371). These people, however, have no use whatsoever for poetry; they demand to be entertained with 'the buffoonery of clowns' (II 1372), and move from 'incomprehension' to 'derision' to 'anger' to 'unleashed fury' (II 1374–5) in which they kill three of the actors, including the leader of the company: 'men have destroyed Poetry in the world' (II 1375).

The other clash, between two ways of conceiving the nature and ends of poetry, underlies the entire play, a clash between the Scalognati (whose name means 'down on their luck'), who long ago chose to abandon the attempt to breach the philistinism of the bourgeois world and have immersed themselves in the solipsism of an art that reaches no one but its creators – an art abandoned to the irrational, the oneiric, the surreal – and the Thespians, who have exhausted themselves in the effort to bring poetry 'among people' (II 1366).

This company, led by a once well-known actress, Countess Ilse Paulsen, has been reduced, by its obstinate dedication to the task of communicating their poetic text, to extreme frustration, exhaustion, and hunger, and brought close to the threshold of hallucination (II 1321–2). Thus, their arrival at the hallucinatory and oneiric world of the Scalognati's villa seems an almost inevitable destination literally and metaphorically. Pirandello is marvellously successful in creating the sense of a crucial point in their experience, a decisive test, which could be for them the end of a long quest. The language of the entire first act conveys an overwhelming sense of hunger, poverty, exhaustion, even delirium ('like mangy, famished, stray dogs, kicked away by everyone,' II 1324; 'a count with neither a county nor a bank account,' II 1316; 'ragged as a beggar,' II 1327; 'She's so tired she can't stand up any more,' II 1316; 'She's feverish, delirious,' II 1319; etc.), and a powerful sense of an impending end ('the last remains of our company,' II 1315; 'the last ounce of strength,' II 1317; 'now that we've reached the end,' II 1320), of the imminent conclusion of the quest that has led the Thespians to this final destination, conveyed by Ilse's Dantean reference to their experience as 'this sea we've crossed' (II 1326).

With equal power Pirandello succeeds in creating the sensation of an existence on the threshold between everyday reality and another mysterious, magical, dreamlike world. The acting company senses it immediately in the solitude and strangeness of the place, but, strongly linked, as they still are, to everyday reality, they try to explain the apparitions, created by the Scalognati 'to scare people and keep them away,' in realistic terms; they interpret them as 'signals you gave us to let us know we'd finally reached our destination' (II 1315). But the Scalognati interpret the arrival of the Thespians as well, first as an enemy attack, and then as a form of entertainment organized by their leader Cotrone ('Ah, we get it! You've arranged to surprise us with a performance! ...

and they took ours for a performance too!' II 1316). In fact, ambiguity of interpretation is as much at home in the continuous intermingling of reality and dream at the Scalogna villa, where even the external solidity of the walls can evaporate instantly: 'Take this façade. All I have to do is shout ... Hey there! (*Instantly the façade of the villa is lit by a wonderful dawn light*) – and the walls give off light!' (II 1336). Very soon the actors are either enchanted by the magical atmosphere, or at least disturbed by the sense of the supernatural. Ilse is the most resistant to its fascination, and to the fascination of Cotrone's eloquence: 'It is like being at the very borderlines of life here, Countess. The borderlines come undone at will; the invisible enters; phantoms take on shapes of air ... Things happen here that usually happen only in dreams. I make them happen while we are awake ... Dreams, music, prayer, love ... all that man is, you will find within and around this villa' (II 1337). This borderline between reality and dream is the perfect setting for the progressive seduction of the acting troupe, still strongly attached to the idea that poetry 'must live among people,' by the inhabitants of the magic world of the Scalogna villa.

The seduction takes place in various stages. At the end of the first act all Ilse's friends have been seduced, some spurred by their hunger ('*Battaglia*: We've got to have something to eat!' II 1331), or by their fatigue ('*Cromo*: Well, at least we'd have a roof over our heads! You don't want to stay here in the damp of the night, do you?' ibid.), most by Cotrone's eloquence. They enter the villa, but Ilse continues to resist and will enter only at the end of the second act, during which Cotrone will exhaust all his resources as a magician in command of strange apparitions, but especially as a magician of words, to persuade her to take refuge in a world in which poetry is lusory and solipsistic, seeking no end beyond play. He begins with the concrete offer of the best bedroom in the villa (II 1335), and goes on to the wonderful spectacle of the dawn light on the front walls of the villa ('*Ilse [amazed like a little girl]*: Oh, how beautiful!' II 1336); to the mysterious voices interjected into La Sgricia's account of the original apparition of the Angel Onehundredone 'with his holy escort' ('*Ilse [shaken]*: What world is this? and these voices?' II 1340), an apparition that now occurs every night at the villa; to the extraordinary entrance of the young actor Spizzi 'costumed as a young poet, resembling the one who killed himself for the countess' (II 1342; the author of the poetic text the company has been performing); to the promise of a performance of the 'Tale of the Changeling' (the text in question). But it is above all with his eloquence that he seeks to persuade

Ilse of the legitimacy of their dedication to a lusory poetry which is an end unto itself:

> We will perform your 'Tale of the Changeling' too like a marvel sufficient in itself, asking nothing from anyone anymore ... What are you still looking for from people? Can't you see what you've gotten from them so far? (II 1346)

Cotrone understands Ilse's passion, which he once shared:

> So this work – played before ordinary people – because it's the work of a poet – has been your ruin?! Oh, how well I understand! ... When I say 'the work of a poet' it's not to disparage it – quite the contrary! – It's to disparage the people who turned their back on it! ... I hate such people! That's why I live here. (II 1328–9)

He has renounced it in favour of a life of self-sufficient creativity, a life devoted to the creation of visions that are addressed to no one and seek no dialogue with anyone:

> You actors give flesh to visions so they may live – and they do live! We do the opposite: we make visions out of our flesh, and we too make them live as well. We don't have to seek them far away – we need only make them emerge from ourselves. You called yourself only a shadow of what you once were? ... Well, whatever you once were, you've only to let her out. Don't you think she's still alive inside you? Isn't the spirit of the young man who killed himself for you alive still? You have him inside you. (II 1341–2)

External reality undergoes the same process of transformation into fantasy: 'With these friends of mine I contrive to diffuse even exterior reality into a soft glow, by pouring the soul, like wisps of painted clouds, into the dreaming night' (II 1344). Though invented as a game ('We are on holiday here,' II 1323), these phantoms, he claims, are just as authentic as poetic works that are meant to communicate with others:

> I have always invented truths ... one is never more truthful than when one invents truth. (II 1342)

> I have never done anything else all my life ... All those truths we refuse to recognize consciously, I make them emerge from the secret places of our

84 . Living Masks

senses, or – in other cases, the more frightening ones – from the recesses of
our instincts ... Now, in this place, I endeavour to dissolve them into eva-
nescent visions, passing shadows. (II 1343–4)

It is no longer a game, but a marvellous reality in which we live, cut off
from everything, to the excess of madness. (II 1345)

And here perhaps lies the real obstacle to Ilse's acceptance of his proposal, in this defence of a detachment from the fundamental human
needs for understanding and communication. Cotrone concludes his
peroration with an invitation to join him on this holiday from either, to
be satisfied with this haven: 'Well, I extend to you the greeting that used
to be proffered to pilgrims: unlace your sandals, set down your staff.
You have reached the end of your quest' (II 1345), and convinces Ilse to
enter the villa too, at least for the night, since 'the night belongs to
dreams' (II 1346). During the night, which occupies the entire third act,
the process of seduction intensifies and Cotrone's magic reaches its
greatest heights. All leave their sleeping bodies (II 1351, 1356–7) and
with extraordinary clarity see their own dreams and desires, their hidden needs, take on form and come alive. The rear wall disappears and
the march of the Angel Onehundredone with his entire cohort reoccurs
(II 1352–3). Spizzi hangs himself from a tree in the garden beyond
because of his secret love for the countess, to everyone's horror ('Please,
Countess, don't be frightened. It's the villa. It comes alive like this
every night, spontaneously, in music and in dreams. And dreams take
on a life of their own outside us, without our knowing it,' II 1359). All
the minor characters needed for the performance of the 'Tale of the
Changeling' are waiting as life-size stuffed dolls in the prop room or
'apparition arsenal,' ready to come alive; all the musical instruments
needed stand ready to play by themselves; the major characters come in
dressed for the parts while their bodies are asleep in their rooms; the
women who are to play the part of the 'two neighbours' appear out of
nowhere evoked by the passion and intensity of the performance. Then
Cotrone will make his final attempt to convince Ilse. 'I wanted to show
you that your *Tale* can live only here' (II 1366), he says, as at the end of
the second act he had promised he would, though without obtaining
her assent. 'I understand that the countess cannot give up her mission
... Not even you want the work to live by itself – in the way it could only
here,' he had said; to which Ilse had replied: 'It lives in me, but that is

not enough! it must live among people!' (II 1346). At the end of the third
act too, Cotrone must admit that he has failed to convince Ilse: 'But you
insist on taking the play out to mankind. So be it!' At which point, as if
by a desperate act of seductive magic, 'the powerful rumbling of the
cavalcade of the Mountain Giants is heard ... The walls of the villa
shake ... They all stay there listening arrested in fear' (II 1366). But not
even this deters Ilse from her unswerving purpose.

Throughout these scenes, much more powerfully than in the 'intermezzi' of *Each in His Own Way*, Pirandello explores the potential of the
stage space, which he had so boldly liberated in *Six Characters*, and his
imagination makes use of it in creative and revolutionary ways. In the
opening scenes of *Six Characters* the stage had been freed of all the con-
strictions of the bourgeois drama, of the suffocating walls of the bourgeois parlour that had so long been a prison not only for the souls of the
characters, but above all for the creativity and imagination of the dramatists. On that liberated stage the encounter between the Pirandellian
characters and their antagonists had taken place. On that liberated stage
a new Pirandellian play had been in rehearsal. To that liberated stage the
Pirandellian characters had come in search of an author. But since the
actors, frustrated by a play they found incomprehensible, were longing
for a good old-fashioned play, and the six characters thought that their
drama was the family melodrama they were 'bringing' with them,
all too soon that liberated stage had yielded to the clutter of the scenery
and props of the conventional theatre, of Madame Pace's establishment
and the Father's house and garden. In *The Mountain Giants*, instead, the
stage space is explored innovatively and imaginatively as an integral
element of Pirandello's dramatic language.

There would seem to be two fundamental reasons why the major
Pirandellian character of this play, and her troupe in turn, cannot ac-
cede to the idea of an exclusively lusory and solipsistic art. One is
clearly the fundamental, irrepressible human need of all Pirandellian
characters, from the author's earliest works, for human communication, the persistent search for some assent from their social environment even when – or especially when – society is unwilling to
recognize the individual's different truth, his unique personal identity,
the very existence of a right to a private truth. The Scalognati want to
do entirely without the recognition of others ('Do you really need the
others to believe in you in order to believe in yourself?' II 1314); they
preach total self-sufficiency:

It would be good for you to follow our example a bit ... to do without everything and to need nothing. (II 1331)

We are masters here. Masters of nothing and of everything ... You can't have everything, except when you've got nothing any more ... [Instead] you still want something. When you no longer want anything, then yes. (II 1344)

But the Thespians refuse to relinquish their need for communication and recognition. When Cotrone says of his material poverty: 'We may lack the necessities, but we have such an abundance of all superfluities ...' (II 1336), he is speaking of the scarcity of daily bread, but we may well apply his 'necessities' figuratively to what for the Thespians is an absolutely necessary component of art, its communicative function.

The second reason for their rejection of Cotrone's view of art is the irrational character of his poetry and the detachment he claims to be content with. Reason is the death of poetry, according to Cotrone ('You are not turning rational on me, are you? Down with reason!' II 1313); the freedom and poetic creativity of the detached life at the villa are a direct result of the exclusion of rationality:

With crazy people anything's possible. (II 1314)

And these voices!? Accept them! Don't try to explain them! ... If they help you to enter another truth, far from your own, even one so transient and mutable as this ... stay, stay in that far distance and try to look at things with the eyes of this little old lady who has seen the Angel. One must stop reasoning. That is the basis of our life here. Lacking everything, but with all the time in the world: an incalculable treasure, a welling of countless dreams. The things around us speak and have meaning only in the arbitrary forms into which our desperation happens to change them. (II 1340)

He argues for the suppression of reason in favour of a return to a child's innocence and openness ('One cannot make these marvels happen out of mere curiosity! One must believe in them, my friend, as children do,' II 1362; 'Learn from the children, as I said before, who make up a game and then believe in it, and live it as if it were real!' II 1366). The Pirandellian characters, by contrast, consumed by the need to understand, to search for truth, to analyse it, to get to the root of their suffering, despite the opacity and impenetrability of reality, refuse to give

up the quest – which yields more anguish than knowledge. The attempt
to explain reality rationally responds to an irrepressible human need in
them, as irrepressible as the need to communicate, however meagre the
results may be.

In *The Mountain Giants* Pirandello poses the question of the nature
and function of art, examines its ostensibly contradictory tendencies,
the lusory and solipsistic as opposed to the communicative, and asks
whether the choice of the Scalognati means an enhancement or a dimi-
nution of the essence of the work of art and of humanity. He concludes
that it entails an impoverishment of both, the loss of an essential human
dimension, which man is already in danger of losing in a mass industrial society.

Yet after siding with Ilse in insisting on the essence and function of
art as communication, Pirandello in the sketchy outline we have of the
fourth act intended us to witness the destruction of this kind of poetry
at the hands of the helots of modern society, perhaps to suggest that
unfortunately only the other kind of art, an art that is merely play and
has no reference beyond itself, an art stripped of all vital communicative function, may be able to survive in that mass society.

In *The New Colony* and *Lazarus* Pirandello had dramatized the quest
for new certainties and for paths to renewal and regeneration. *The
New Colony* touches on the possibility of universal love as a source
of renewal for mankind when new forms of social organization have
failed; *Lazarus* centres on this possibility, if not altogether convincingly.
The Mountain Giants, on the other hand, explores the nature of art as
communication, as a quest not for renewal but for a kind of last life-
line, for another kind of certitude, as to whether the truth of a work of
art can be created – or discovered – and communicated. The outcome
of this quest is dismaying: just as the human need for communication,
though irrepressible, remains extremely difficult if not impossible to
satisfy, so the communicative impulse of poetry, though essential and
inalienable, is blunted by its target, a humanity progressively more deaf
and resistant to art.

It is impossible to be absolutely sure what final form the action and
dialogue would have taken had Pirandello had time to write the entire
fourth act, which he told his son Stefano he had worked out in his mind
'during the entire next to last night of his life' (II 1371). With this reser-
vation in mind, it seems appropriate that, in the words of Stefano's outline, after Ilse's death, her friends would shout 'that men have
destroyed Poetry in the world' (II 1375); and that Cotrone, seeing the

imminent danger, 'tries for the last time to persuade them to desist; passionately he reminds them of the happiness they are turning their backs
on, the night of enchantment at the villa, when all the spirits of poetry
had come so naturally to life in them, and could continue to live, if they
would only return and remain there forever' (II 1374). It seems appropriate that Cotrone would comment that both 'the poor fanatical servants of life' and 'the fanatical servants of Art' are irremediably enslaved to their respective tyrants (II 1375), and that he would blame the
crime on the latter rather than the former. For 'the fanatics of Art, who
think themselves the sole repositories of the spirit' (II 1374), should
have known better than 'the poor fanatical servants of life, in whom
today the spirit is mute' and who in their ignorance 'have innocently
broken, like rebellious puppets, the fanatical servants of Art. Artists
who do not know how to speak to men because they have cut themselves off from life, though not enough to be content solely with their
own dreams; they still insist on imposing them on those who have
other things to do than believe in them' (II 1375). According to Cotrone,
that is, the artist has cut himself off from life by the very fact of becoming an artist, and can no longer communicate with those 'in whom
today the spirit is mute'; he might as well accept the solipsism of the
Scalognati as a solution. But the Thespians do not consider themselves
'cut off from life,' and in their stubborn yearning for communication
they affirm that the authentic Pirandellian character, even when confronted with the evidence of the impossibility of communication, will
never cease to assert the need for it, which is experienced as an insuppressible truth. To recall once more the condition of the souls in Dante's
limbo, the dying of 'hope' does not quench the 'desire'; if the evidence
on one side leads to despair, the irrepressible need on the other leads to
the refusal to give up an important human dimension, to deny a human
truth.

What in Cotrone's statement is inconsistent with the resolution of the
play, as sketched in Stefano's recollections, is the proposition that while
in these 'poor fanatical servants of life ... today the spirit is mute,' it
'may, still, speak some day' (II 1375). Unless we consider Cotrone as a
kind of new variant on the Pirandellian character, in that while the others, confronted with the harsh evidence of reality, can no longer go on
nourishing their hope but cannot relinquish their desire, in Cotrone, the
sworn enemy of rationality, who has been able for so long to suppress
desire, hope has not yet wholly died.

8 Pirandello in Our Time

> The extent of even this partial list of influences marks Pirandello as the
> most seminal artist of our time.
>
> (Robert Brustein, *Theater of Revolt*, p. 316)

One of the most important writers of the twentieth century, Pirandello
is one of the primary sources of its thought and its literature, and unquestionably the primary source of twentieth-century theatre. Without
him there may well have been no experimental or avant-garde theatre
during the thirties and forties, no Epic Theatre, no existentialist theatre,
no Theatre of the Absurd,[1] no Living Theatre.[2] His work continues to
influence playwrights, fiction writers, and film-makers to this day.

There are at least two reasons for Pirandello's profound influence, an
influence far more enduring than that of his perhaps more sensational
successors. To make a somewhat old-fashioned distinction, we might
see the two reasons in terms of content and form: one having to do with
the accuracy and depth of his insight into the crisis of modern man and
modern culture, the other with the innovative stylistic brilliance with
which he portrayed that crisis.

In its penetration and power Pirandello's work achieved a vitality
and universality that make its portrayal of the human condition altogether relevant today. Pirandello was the writer who best understood
the serious crisis bourgeois culture underwent during the years of
peace and apparent economic prosperity between the 1890s and the
first tragic world conflict. D'Annunzio, an equally prolific writer more
widely known both in Italy and abroad in his time, also attempted to

express that crisis, but came nowhere near Pirandello in understanding its nature and depth. Sensing the eclipse of the heroic ideals of the Risorgimento period just ended, intuiting the resentment of a younger generation compelled to settle down to the prosaic task of administering the meagre resources of the country instead of pursuing heroic deeds on the battlefields where their elders had supposedly covered themselves with glory during the struggle for the country's reunification, D'Annunzio tried to exalt the gospel of 'action,' to keep alive the myth of the 'inimitable life' and of war as its highest expression, the ultimate cleanser of the malaise of life in bourgeois society – a myth of whose falseness all D'Annunzio's readers would become aware at the first engagements on the harsh front of everyday reality and the First World War.[3]

By contrast Pirandello, as noted in the introductory chapter, understood perfectly that the comfortable stability and self-confidence the bourgeois world had enjoyed had disappeared forever during that crucial quarter of a century; that the new generation was by now assailed by doubts as to its very identity and the possibility of ever getting a grip on it, let alone of communicating it in a normal, functioning relationship with society; that man in the new century had lost, in sum, the sense of unity, of a community of beliefs and values, the faith in the ability to communicate them to others, which the nineteenth-century world had amply enjoyed. He understood that the bourgeois intellectual saw his role becoming increasingly irrelevant the further the national uprising of the mid-century receded into the past and the more the political and trade-unionist mass movements of the proletariat grew on the left, the industrial baronies on the right. Pirandello understood that he felt betrayed in the very certainties the earlier bourgeois world had enjoyed: the certainty of the omnipotence of scientific knowledge, which no longer seemed to have kept its promises; the pride and confidence in the principles and institutions that ruled the social behaviour of that world, which no longer seemed capable of hiding its mediocrity and its gradual disintegration.

Pirandello dramatized the bewilderment caused by the revelation of the meanness, the pretentiousness, the hypocrisy of petit bourgeois ideals; he dramatized the impossibility of holding on to the unified vision of reality which that society had fostered, once the old values and ideals had been degraded and rejected; he dramatized – after the fragmentation and decay of the intellectual, ethical, and social components of a historical era – the collapse of the certainties and assumptions regarding the individual himself, the integrity of the person, his very identity. He created characters compelled to face both the disintegration of the social reality in which they had lived all their lives, and the disintegration of the certainties regarding their identity and personal worth, characters who passionately protest the loss of form, of unity, of the certainty of their own identity and of its communicability – an irreparable loss that is the essence of their existential condition and the cause of their insoluble conflict with life in our time.

With such a reading of this cultural crisis, Pirandello did far more than dramatize the malaise of the bourgeoisie at the turn of the century: he raised that critical experience to universal terms, translated it into a representation of the fundamental conflicts besetting humanity in our time. Hence Pirandello's themes are the recurring themes of its major philosophical and literary-artistic currents: the themes of solitude and alienation, of the tension between the need for individual freedom and self-affirmation and for social integration, with its demand for a degree of conformity; the themes of the challenge to all absolutes and of the recognition of the subjectivity of all beliefs. The depth and truth of Pirandello's assessment of our cultural crisis, and thus the modernity and universality of his themes, have caused great numbers of thinkers and artists to turn for inspiration to his work at every critical turn of our cultural history.

To get a clearer picture of the scope of Pirandello's influence, it might be useful to first shed light on some claims of 'Pirandellism' that need clarification or rebuttal. Scholars have managed to find in the history of Western culture, going as far back as the Greek and Latin classics down to Cervantes and Marivaux, Manzoni and Verga,[4] a few thematic and stylistic elements they consider typical of 'Pirandellism' – most of them clearly outlined by Pirandello himself in his essays, particularly in *L'umorismo*. They point out that in Galdos' *El amigo manso* a character rises from the writer's inkwell; or that one of Unamuno's characters threatens his author to commit suicide;[5] or that young Ramón Gómez de la Serna between 1909 and 1912 published, in literary magazines with a minimal circulation, plays such as *The Uninhabited Palace*, *The Madman*, and *Theatre of Solitude*, which were never performed, and which when they were published in his complete works years later he titled collectively 'dead theatre,' Pirandellian plays *ante litteram*, especially those in which the nature of drama is discussed in a way vaguely reminiscent of Dr Hinkfuss. But the fact remains that while the work of Pirandello had enormous cultural resonance, the occasional 'Pirandellisms' of these writers went so unnoticed that their discovery is always a surprise to the discoverers themselves.

At times what scholars take as instances of Pirandellism are only aspects of the crisis of the traditional bourgeois and naturalistic nineteenth-century theatre with which in fact Pirandello himself had to deal. Thus, Claudio Vicentini reminds us that Mallarmé led the Symbolistes in a discussion of how inadequate, even detrimental, actors, directors, and staging were to the communication of a poetic text; hence their preference for the reading over the staged performance of dramatic texts. On the other hand, he sees many experiments attempted from Stanislavsky to Meyerhold to Gordon Craig, which relied on elaborate staging and disregarded the written text, as antecedents of Pirandello's clearing of the stage in *Six Characters* or the treatment of the textual question in *Tonight We Improvise*. Vicentini maintains that the kind of theatrical action envisioned in the manifesto of Marinetti's 'Teatro sintetico futurista' as a 'training ground of the spectators for war' was inspired by the same reasons that led Pirandello to abandon fiction for the theatre.[6] But while the crisis of bourgeois culture and of its theatre was a question confronted by many, Pirandello did so in a manner unmistakably his own: he certainly never thought of eliminating actors or directors, stage or staging, least of all the poetic text. All his dramatic works are conceived in terms intended to subvert the basic canons of bourgeois and naturalistic theatre, as we have seen beginning with the discussion of *Liolà*, and Pirandello certainly did not need any help from futurism, let alone to have his way cleared for him by the futurists.

In fact, although a number of critics take pleasure in searching for connections between the enormous body of Pirandello's work and the theories and output of the futurists,[7] the inevitably scant results never add to or subtract from his richness and revolutionary originality; a sure instance of the influence of futurism on Pirandello can neither be documented historically nor pinpointed in the texts. He observed the movement with attentive interest, but deliberately steered clear of it, considering himself a serious writer and literary futurism a phenomenon of immaturity; at most, being a good friend of many futurist sympathizers, he took part in their games on rare occasions.[8] That is, when futurism came upon the Italian literary scene, Pirandello was not an easily influenced beginner still in search of direction; he was the mature, successful author of a great number of short stories, among them many acknowledged masterpieces, of several highly original novels, and of a few plays already genuinely innovative in theme and structure. When the tiny group of young futurists started shouting that it was high time to be done with the archaeology of classicism and to kill the Romantics' moonlight, Pirandello was perfectly well aware that they were barking at shadows, and that he himself had been a major, indeed the major, cause of the final eclipse of the classic-romantic literary remnants of the nineteenth century. When Marinetti published the first futurist manifesto in the *Figaro* of 22 February 1909, Pirandello was enjoying extraordinary professional success and was so immersed in his work that he could hardly have had much time to spare for the noisy productions of the futurists. *The Late Mattia Pascal*, 1904, had reaped such an international success (it had been translated into several languages during the intervening years) that Pirandello, besides continuing to write for *Marzocco* and *Nuova Antologia*, had begun to write for the *Trisettimanale politico e militare* and the *Corriere della sera*, and had begun to publish with the prestigious publishing house of the Treves brothers. The years 1907–8 had been successful ones for his career in other ways. He had won a university chair, a full professorship at the Magistero section of the University of Rome. He had published the two essays crucial to the success of the competition for the chair, *L'umorismo* and *Arte e scienza*, which had led to a polemical exchange with Benedetto Croce. And during the years in which Marinetti had written his first manifestos and tried to associate often reluctant writers, painters, and architects with the movement, Pirandello had written and rewritten the work most removed from futurist aesthetics, the historical novel *I vecchi e i giovani*, first published serially in *Rassegna contemporanea* in 1909 and considerably reworked for publication in 1913 with Treves Brothers. While the futurists were presenting their poetic readings in the theatres of Italy's major cities, often like veritable theatrical 'happenings,' with posters, advertisements, deliberate provocations to fistfights on the sidewalks and to shouting matches and booing in the pit, Pirandello was writing the short stories of *La vita nuda*, a collection as important within the context of both his fiction and his plays as it is removed from any aspect of futurism. And the theatrical company most removed from futurism to be found in Italy at the time, the company of Nino Martoglio, was performing in Rome *La morsa* and *Lumie di Sicilia* (one written way back in 1898, one contemporary), the two plays of Pirandello closest to the bourgeois theatre and most remote from futurism in theme and resolution, which reveal, that is, that as a dramatist too (as earlier as a writer of fiction) Pirandello was tilling ground uniquely his own, already creating works of considerable originality, and was surely not waiting to be told what themes – and least of all what style – the future literature of Italy demanded, especially not by the cultural demagogues of the manifestos, who had yet to produce anything of truly artistic value, who had not proposed nor could propose either themes compatible with Pirandello's vision or forms suitable to their expression. Pirandello was the true creator and innovator; the futurists were as yet only cultural agitators.

Pirandello never entertained the juvenile idea that to express the severe crisis of the turn of the century a writer had to surrender to chaos, or that to express the energy of the locomotive or the speed of the racing car it was necessary, let alone sufficient, to eliminate punctuation or abolish syntax or stretch words from one end of the line to the other ('Boooooombaaaardamento / Booooomboooombaaaaardaaamento').[9] Pirandellian ideas and forms were effectively revolutionary because the former were truly original and the latter genuinely expressive of that originality, particularly because it was an originality that had developed gradually from within a tradition, had made use of the motifs and forms of that tradition. Even when he was out to demonstrate that the tradition was no longer valid, that it had to go, he did not decree its death through the publication of a manifesto that required artists to start from zero and build on nothing. The Pirandello who disparaged the myths of the positivistic age and the art that had celebrated them, particularly the bourgeois theatre, was able to proclaim their falseness by endowing his characters with the appearances and values of that theatre, instead of rejecting them outright, instead of 'burning the museums' of that literature. He placed his characters in situations recognizable as those of the bourgeois theatre, making them wear its clothing and speak its language to condemn its conventionality. He made them embody figures of the bourgeois world to protest its alienating qualities; made them argue passionately, as bourgeois characters had argued in defence of bourgeois conventions, against the hypocrisy of those conventions; made them proclaim, using the modes of bourgeois communication, both their condemnation to incommunicability and their insuppressible need to communicate. In short, he made use of traditional theatre (and the world it reflected) to discredit it, just as he used it to demonstrate the validity of new, experimental, open forms. Pirandello was a great innovator because he never dreamed of 'burning museums' and 'killing the moonlight,' and achieved his revolution, instead, one step at a time, logically, consistently. Like the great writers and the true revolutionaries of all ages, Pirandello used to revolutionary ends all sorts of antiques and archaeological treasures, from a faithful reproduction of a bourgeois plot like the sentimental family melodrama of *Six Characters* to an archaeological piece like the historical reconstruction of *Henry IV*, and perhaps no one has ever used 'moonlight' more frequently and with less romantic sentimentality than the way Pirandello used it in 'Ciaula' and in many similar dramatic situations in his fiction.

Thus, during the years of the manifestos of futurism's short creative season it is difficult to trace any genuine futurist influence in Pirandello's work. For instance, when the 1912 technical manifesto of futurist literature was circulating and groups like that of Mayakovsky or the cubo-futurists began to organize in faraway Russia, Pirandello collected in two volumes (*Terzetti*, 1912; *La trappola*, 1915) about fifty stories written between 1912 and 1915 that completely ignore futurism, and the Treves brothers did not consider the re-publication of *I vecchi e i giovani* (1913) an anachronism. And when finally the manifestos of 'futurist synthetic theatre' were published, in 1915, Pirandello was writing *Pensaci Giacomino, Il berretto a sonagli*, and *Liolà* (all staged with great success by Angelo Musco in 1916). In 1917 came *Cosí è, se vi pare* and *Il piacere dell'onestà*. These are all works that, though they mark a decisive turning away from the modes of naturalism (even according to the critics who persist in affirming the existence of a naturalistic Pirandello), reveal no trace of the modes of futurism, and their action still unfolds, for the most part, in the traditional, orderly bourgeois parlour.

And when the war was over, in the year of *Il giuoco delle parti, Ma non è una cosa seria*, and the Treves short story collection, *Un cavallo nella luna*, it is debatable whether there still existed a futurist epoch, a futurist influence, a futurist avant-garde. There remained, rather, a futurism that continued to repeat itself for years on end, whose events were staged increasingly rarely, and then as relics, archaeology, curiosities.[10] The theatrical works were almost always conceived as 'microhappenings,' and were attended primarily by the futurists involved and some of their closest friends, who came out of courtesy as one goes to the opening of a friend's personal show, to make it seem well attended; a scattering of the public came not to listen to the texts but to enjoy the shouting and taunting. By the war's end futurism in painting, in which it had inspired considerably greater originality than in literature,[11] was replaced by metaphysical painting first and surrealism a bit later; in architecture the dull, sober, banal public works of the Fascist period confined the futurist projects of Sant'Elia exclusively to his sketchbooks; in literature very little of the themes and forms invoked by the futurists survived. Perhaps some rather threadbare ideas, like activism, machismo, anti-feminism, continued to circulate among a few survivors seeking the favour of those who proclaimed the new political order. As for Pirandello's works, even in those written during a more narrowly conceived heyday of futurism (1909–18), it is practically impossible to trace any of its influence.

In fact, one need only examine the first futurist manifesto point by point to realize its remoteness from the poetic world of Pirandello.[12] Can we conceive of a Pirandello who 'sings' 'the love of danger,' 'daring, rebellion,' 'the aggressive gesture,' 'the slap in the face, the fist,' 'the beauty of speed,' 'the roaring automobile,' 'the aggressive character,' 'eternally omnipresent speed,' 'great crowds aroused by work, pleasure, revolt'?; a Pirandello who 'glorifies' 'war – the only cleanser of the world – militarism, patriotism, ... contempt for woman'? One need only examine the later 'technical' manifesto of futurist literature point by point and try to imagine a Pirandello who 'lines up nouns as casually as they come to mind,' or 'uses verbs only in the infinitive,' 'eliminates adjectives, adverbs, punctuation,' or uses 'all nouns only' in tandem, 'man-torpedoboat, woman-gulf,' or indulges in entire 'chains of analogies,' or 'orchestrates images, lining them up according to a *maximum of disorder*,' or 'eliminates the "I" from literature, that is, eliminates psychology altogether,' or 'abolishes [man] from literature, finally replacing him with matter.' Again one need only examine the numerous manifestos on a futurist theatre,[13] and try to imagine a Pirandello who has learned 'contempt for the audience,' 'the pleasure of being booed,' 'the horror of instant success'; a Pirandello who uses the theatre to 'induce warlike feelings in the Italian soul'; who embraces the 'synthetic theatre' tenet that each act of a play must be reduced to 'a few seconds,' to no more than 'moments'; who tries to 'make them [his audience] forget the monotony of daily life, by forcing them through a *labyrinth of sensations inspired by the most extreme originality and combined in the most unforeseeable ways*'; who is determined to 'abolish all technique,' to 'keep clear of all deforming cultural intrusions,' to 'abolish comedy, drama, tragedy.' Of course, in fifty pages of precepts and commands we might expect to find a few that seem relevant to Pirandello, such as the notion that 'the scenic action must invade pit and spectators.' But what the futurists meant by such invasions – the uncontrolled mayhem, that is, by which they gauged their ratings (it is clear from the reviews collected by Antonucci that the public at futurist evenings went not to listen to the texts being read, let alone the long-winded prefaces to the texts, but to enjoy themselves booing, shouting, and carousing), since when the mayhem ceased, the play invariably fell flat – has little to do with the thoroughly controlled 'invasion' of the pit and the spectators realized by Pirandello in *Each in His Own Way*.

Those critics who tend to see futurism everywhere base their assertion of its influence on Pirandello (which as we have noted can be documented neither historically nor textually) in part on a very brief collaboration between Pirandello and the futurist director Anton Giulio Bragaglia, which cannot lead to any such conclusion. In 1923 Bragaglia directed his company in a production of Pirandello's one-act play, *The Man with a Flower in His Mouth*, whereas such masterpieces as *Six Characters*, *Henry IV*, *All'uscita*,[14] and *To Clothe the Naked* had recently been staged – as, for that matter, all his plays had always been – by traditional companies and actors, often even of the old bourgeois and naturalistic school, even of the regional, dialectal school. (Martoglio and his company staged *The Vise* and *Sicilian Limes* in 1910, and *The License* in 1919; Musco presented *Pensaci Giacomino* and *Liolà* in 1916, *The Jinglebell Cap* and *La giara* in 1917; Ruggeri *The Pleasure of Honesty* in 1917, *Il giuoco delle parti* in 1918, *Tutto per bene* in 1920, *Henry IV* in 1922; Emma Gramatica *Ma non è una cosa seria* in 1918 and *La signora Morli* in 1920; Virgilio Talli *Right You Are, if You Think You Are* in 1917, *The Graft* in 1919; other interpreters included Gandusio, Falconi, and Marco Praga. Even the revolutionary *Six Characters* was staged, in 1921, by the traditionalist Niccodemi and his company, to whom Pirandello would also entrust the equally revolutionary *Each in His Own Way* in 1924.) Among them all not even the shadow of a futurist can be detected. The twelve-page play Bragaglia was given did not in any case lend itself to a futurist interpretation, nor could he have influenced it *a posteriori* anyway, just as there is no indication that he influenced any of Pirandello's subsequent works. A contemporary review states that the play 'was performed with the suggestive staging of Bragaglia in his Teatro degli Indipendenti: a splendid frame without a picture, for the great actor demanded by a text which relies so entirely on words and their secret and hidden resonances was definitely missing.'[15] Later Bragaglia collaborated in the staging of some works performed at the Teatro d'Arte, over the short life of which Pirandello presided as its artistic director.[16]

Virgilio Marchi too worked at the Teatro d'Arte, as a scenographer of *Nostra dea* by Bontempelli, *Bellinda e il mostro* by Cicognani, and Dunsany's *Gli dei della montagna*, all quite modern but definitely not futuristic plays. Verdone claims that by observing Marchi's scenography, Pirandello conceived the 'reliance on stage machinery' that he would display in the epilogue of *The New Colony* and in the 'arsenal of apparitions,' the 'storm' scene, and 'the many light tricks' of *The Mountain Giants*,[17] that is, in two of his final works. Determined to find the influence of the futurists in all innovative aspects of twentieth-century theatre, Verdone flatly attributes these stage effects to futurism, though one might well argue that they were simply an inevitable outcome of the structural evolution of Pirandello's theatre since *Liolà* and his revolutionary use of the stage since *Six Characters*.

Another element frequently mentioned in connection with Pirandello by those who argue for the pervasive influence of futurism is 'simultaneity,' which in futurist paintings consists chiefly in the use of a multiple image to express movement (a technique clearly borrowed from primitive cinematography),[18] and in futurist literature consists in the simultaneous presence of different personalities in the same individual, a motif the futurists unquestionably copied from Pirandello rather than the other way around.

Of course, the futurists insisted that the contrary was true; they often took credit for the whole twentieth-century Italian theatre. For instance, a review in the Turin *Gazzetta del popolo* of 23 October 1921 reports that the night before at the Maffei Theatre Marinetti had said that 'if in Italy a young theatre and more or less young playwrights like Pirandello, Cavacchioli, and Chiarelli exist, who have freed themselves from the old forms and shown a new boldness, it is only thanks to the futurist movement' (Antonucci, p. 159). The wildest claims of this sort were usually made by Francesco Cangiullo. Whenever such boasts were proclaimed onstage before the performance of a futurist play, audiences reacted as if they had heard blasphemy, as we read in a review in *Corriere della sera* of 12 January 1924 of the performance of the night before:

> The storm exploded when Cangiullo discussed the fundamental tenets of the futurist theatre and asserted that Pirandello, Chiarelli, Cavacchioli, and the avant-garde playwrights of the regular theatres have done nothing but plagiarize the futurists. The spectators howled in all keys and whistled derisively through their door keys, and Marinetti had to come out to back Cangiullo up. (Antonucci, pp. 191–2)

Ettore Romagnoli wrote in the Bolognese magazine *In platea*:

The new theatrical year has begun life well. It was born all pink and white, and lively, tripping along gaily on its little futurist legs, at the Saint Martin Theatre. One of its godfathers, Cangiullo, managed to proclaim over the audience's carnival din: 'Futurism is the father of all contemporary theatre.' A chorus of protest from the audience, then a lone voice: 'Out with the names!' and Cangiullo: 'Pirandello!' The shouts of protest rise to the heavens of the Primum Mobile, to the celestial thrones and dominions. It is impossible to understand why the audience should suddenly be seized by such an acute excess of loyalty to Pirandello; and the Royal Constables must intervene. (Antonucci, p. 189)

Romagnoli does not understand the reason for this 'acute excess' because he is an avowed futurist ('I am saying, then, that the tenets of futurism coincide perfectly with the principles of common sense'; ibid., p. 190) and does not doubt that simultaneity was invented by Marinetti: 'If one analyses his [Pirandello's] works, one finds, in fact, that he puts certain futurist principles into practice. Simultaneity, for instance: a truly brilliant invention of Marinetti' (ibid.).[19]

Adriano Tilgher, less convinced of this futurist paternity, limits himself to observing that perhaps the one merit of the 'futurist synthetic theatre' was that of 'clearing the way for Pirandello,' and that 'the time has come to recognize that the aims of futurist theatre have been realized more in the stage settings and the theatrical currents that since 1916 ("grottesco," Rosso, Bontempelli, Pirandello, etc.) have succeeded each other on the Italian stage, than in the dramatic works of the founder of futurism' (Antonucci, p. 282).

Mario Ferrigni, in his review of Marinetti's *Simultanina* for *L'illustrazione Italiana*, is convinced that Pirandello et al. have done it better and sooner: 'The idea [of the simultaneous presence of different personalities in one character] is muddled and definitely not new: it has found more complex and more solid theatrical expression in Pirandello, Bontempelli, Rosso di San Secondo' (Antonucci, p. 294). Simultanina, in Ferrigni's words,

is a female character who may embody Woman, as much as Life, or Love ... She is surrounded, courted, and desired by many male figures, the Gourmet, the Sportsman, the Bibliophile, the Professor-poet, the Con-man, the Dongiovanni-journalist. For the Gourmand this woman is cuisine, food, and flavour; for the Sportsman she is strength, violence, play; for the confidence man she is intrigue, seduction, revolution, chaos; for the Scholar

she is sterile contemplation, books, ... and so on. Simultanina then is supposed to be all these things at once and possess all these qualities and possibilities together, to 'be and have everything' ... but she is not a real
woman ... she is life as each one would like to mould it for himself; she is
love as each would like to enjoy it ... she is a stock character, not in the
eighteenth-century sense, but modernized into the figure of the mannequin, to which the words of other people lend a certain look, a certain
stance, even a certain movement. (Antonucci, p. 294)

In the end Simultanina 'slips through everybody's fingers' as Giovanetti's review adds (ibid., p. 290), and although she kills herself 'to
escape her suitors ... she does not die,' Ferrigni concludes (ibid., p. 295).
    But even disregarding the critics' evaluation of *Simultanina*[20] (actually
their unanimous criticism of Marinetti's failure could be used to praise
Pirandello's way of dramatizing the same motif), the futurist play was
first staged in 1931, while 'simultaneity' and multiple personality are
motifs found in the earliest works of Pirandello, in his first novels,
L'esclusa, *Il turno*, *Il fu Mattia Pascal* (written between 1893 and 1903,
when futurism was still far in the future), and soon to be incisively outlined in a passage in *L'umorismo* (1908), which I will have occasion to
quote shortly. Although there are critics today who still see *L'esclusa*
and *Il turno* as exclusively naturalistic works,[21] failing to understand
that no work by Pirandello remains *totally* within the confines of naturalism, a brief consideration reminds us that Marta Ayala and Stellina
are characters who at the end of their respective novels might very well
say what Mrs Ponza says at the end of *Right You Are, if You Think You
Are*, written many years later: that she has been for the characters
around her 'whoever they believe her to be.' Marta Ayala of *L'esclusa* is
one person to her father, another to her mother, another to her husband,
to her colleagues, and never, to them, what she is to herself; hence she is
ostracized when she is an honest woman, and restored to the respect
and the gratitude of her family when she has actually had a sexual
encounter with her supposed lover. Indeed, all the characters around
her are simultaneously themselves and what public opinion and social
pressures want them to be. Stellina in *Il turno* is, like Mrs Ponza, a character who is almost non-existent in herself; she exists only in what she
represents simultaneously to others, that is, to her father the trick card
he plays to accomplish his ingenious sleight of hand, to Alcozer the
means to hold on to his delusion of youth by surrounding himself with
a little 'life,' to the younger suitors what they dream of making her into.

Of the latter, young Alletto, a weaker personality than either Raví or Coppa, is simultaneously what his mother, Raví, Alcozer, and Coppa want him to be. *Il turno* is in fact a novel full of characters who want to pull the strings of the other marionettes: whoever, like Raví, thinks he is the puppet master, in charge of manipulating others' destinies, is himself tricked by fate and chance, and those who are manipulated are always unhappy because they are other than what they would like to be. Old Alcozer dyes his hair, puts on make-up, and marries young women to feel other than what he is because he would like to be other than what he is, not unlike Henry IV many years later. As we watch father, daughter, and suitor busying themselves to help the decrepit husband recover from pneumonia when their plans call for him to die as soon as possible, we realize that already these early Pirandello characters are torn by simultaneous irreconcilable tendencies, dreams, regrets.

We need not dwell at length on the many personalities of Mattia Pascal, in whom coexist simultaneously the public and the private man, the victim and the vindicator of the abuses and greed of Batta Malagna, the devoted son and the major cause of his mother's vulnerable condition, the villain in the eyes of the widow Pescatore and her scapegoat in his own, the lucky gambler and the defenceless exile in an exile to which he is attracted by his luck, the man who expects to be happy when he falls in love and the unhappy lover who is aware that he cannot afford the luxury of falling in love, the returnee freed from his disfiguring eye defect, his financial straits, his youthful immaturity, ready to start a new, more controlled life, and the man reduced to living like a mere shadow of himself, like *the late* Mattia Pascal. Thus, Pirandello gave the concept of simultaneity eloquent expression in important works that antedated by years the futurist manifesto, while the attempts made by the futurists often failed because of their tendency to excessive reduction and simplification, an impoverishment camouflaged with the pretentious new term 'syntheticity.' Pirandello was never attracted by their 'revolutionary' approach; he expressed simultaneity and the multiple personality of his characters with extraordinary dramatic effectiveness, especially in works such as *Henry IV* and *Each in His Own Way*, even as he conveyed the idea that art, as the Father of *Six Characters* laments, freezes the constant change, the endless flux of life, simplifies and reduces the multiplicity and simultaneity that are the richness of life.

There can be no doubt that in regard to this motif of the simultaneous presence of many personalities in one person, whose paternity Marinetti and his acolytes were so eager to claim for themselves, Pirandello had preceded them by more than a decade. He was, if anything, the influence. It was above all the depth and power of Pirandello's understanding of the crisis of man and society in our time that led great numbers of thinkers and artists, including to some extent the futurists themselves, to turn to his work for inspiration. Scholars have traced the extensive connections between the basic themes of Pirandello and the ideas of such representatives of contemporary existentialism as Heidegger, Marcel, Sartre, and Abbagnano.[22] As a notable critic has said, Pirandello, although a man of letters rather than a philosopher, has influenced the thought of our century more than any other contemporary writer.[23]

While his relationship to twentieth-century existentialist thinkers is well established, the equally deep and meaningful relationship between Pirandello's relativism and Giovanni Gentile's 'actualism' and Ugo Spirito's 'problematicism' has been less widely recognized. Gentile poses at the core of his philosophy of actualism the identity of theory and practice, the identity of Vico's *verum est factum*: truth has no transcendental roots, it exists only in history, and in Gentile's lexicon it develops in its 'actuality,' that is, in life, which is a creative act in endless development, in flux, in indefinite progression. As such, truth can only evolve; it cannot be defined once and forever; it does not reside in metaphysical systems, in systems that pretend to explain everything once and for all, for any such system would be invalidated by the creative process of life in which man is immersed.

This central idea of Gentile's actualism is also at the centre of Pirandello's epistemological relativism, of his concept of truth, of the subjectivity, plurality, incompleteness, and continuous evolution of truth. It is the concept expressed so powerfully by the Father of *Six Characters* when he asks the Director whether he does not feel the ground giving way under his feet at the thought that his reality, his truth, will be as different tomorrow from today's as today's is from what it had been in the past; and so dramatically lived by the Pirandellian characters of *Right You Are, if You Think You Are*, each of whom clings tightly to a truth different from that of the others; and so radically experienced by the characters of *Each in His Own Way*, whose truth to their amazement keeps changing in their very hands with each new twist of their multilevelled drama. It is likely that Pirandello, who was familiar with Gentile's thought, drew on it in his own work.

While Pirandello and Gentile were contemporaries, the most impor-

tant philosophical works of Ugo Spirito were published after Pirandello's death, when both his fiction and his plays were widely known.
Obviously Gentile's thought was the major influence on Spirito's philosophy, but it was also as surely leavened by the view of reality dramatized in Pirandello. The basic premises of Spirito's 'problematicism' are
drawn from Hegel's theory of thesis and antithesis that evolve towards
the solution of the synthesis; and from Gentile's theory of the unity of
truth and act, in which pure act cannot be defined because only the creative act itself, or the historical process, defines: if the act, as a developing process, is indefinable, then reality itself defies definition. From
these premises Spirito develops his ideas: that the Hegelian synthesis is
not a definitive conclusion, the quiet haven of an epistemological opti-
mism,[24] but only the thesis of a new antithesis; that the real dialectics is
not thesis–antithesis–synthesis, but a problem and its opposite, problem and contradiction; that life is problematic – life is not truth but
(carrying the logic of Gentile's indefinable truth to its conclusion) an
unending search for truth, for a truth, a certitude, that are, however, in
Pirandello's terms, unreachable. In his view of human reality in our
time Spirito has incorporated the Pirandellian concept that contemporary man has elevated the problematic to the place traditionally occu-
pied by dogma, has lost the certitudes of previous ages and, while he
knows that he cannot retrieve them, does not renounce the search for
them, poses to himself an endless series of questions because to think *is*
to question, to doubt, and doubt is the wellspring of modern consciousness.[25] Spirito, however, unlike Pirandello, does not consider this a loss
to be deplored, but a gain: a world devoid of dogma and certitudes is to
him a richer and more complex world.[26]

Yet for the youth of his time, Spirito realized, the loss of certitudes
creates real difficulties no easier to solve or to live with than they are for
the Pirandellian characters; modern youth must endure the same tragic
condition. 'The historical process implies a ceaseless transformation of
reality and a ceaseless rise of new exigencies that are poorly understood
and accepted by those accustomed to intellectual and moral judgments
which they cannot and do not want to abandon.'[27] From this situation
spring the social alienation, so lethal to hope in the young, which pervades so much of the individual's relationship with his community,
and the identity crisis that afflicts him: the society and culture of our
time wrap such an intricate web of relationships around the individual
that he can no longer see, let alone grasp, reality in its totality, and his
only vision of himself and his world is a fragmentary one. Indeed, Ugo

Spirito's analysis of the human condition of our time and of time to come reads like an index to the suffering of the characters of Pirandello.

Obviously this affinity between Pirandello and Spirito parallels the affinities outlined by many scholars between Pirandello and the existentialists of his own and the following generation, who were thoroughly familiar with Pirandello, as their fiction, plays, and drama criticism amply document.[28] But the influence of Pirandello also pervades the Theatre of the Absurd and the *nouveau roman*, and there are scholars who see it 'alive and present' in Pavese and Bonaviri, in Calvino and Landolfi, in Bassani and Prisco, in Pomilio and Pontiggia, in Sciascia and Samonà, in Bufalino and Tabucchi, in Borges and Cortazàr, in Mann, Musil, and Joyce, in Nabokov and Malraux; it is evident as well in Edward Albee (*The Zoo Story, Who's Afraid of Virginia Woolf, The Sandbox*) and Don DeLillo (*The Day Room*), in Jack Gelber (*The Connection*) and Archibald MacLeish (*J. B., Heracles*), in Harold Pinter (*The Room, The Birthday Party, The Caretaker, The Homecoming, The Dwarfs*) and Dennis Potter (*Pennies from Heaven*), in Tom Stoppard (*Rosencrantz and Guildenstern Are Dead*), in Felipe Alfau (*Locos, Chromos*), in Mario Benedetti (*Ida Y Vuelta*), and in Woody Allen (*The Purple Rose of Cairo*), as well as in the writings of Julian Beck and Judith Malina and in the performances of their Living Theatre, and so on. It is so widespread that one of the scholars who have studied some of these influences finds it necessary to warn us that 'Pirandellism exists even where there is scant familiarity with the works of Pirandello.'[29]

However, the French and German playwrights between the twenties and the sixties on whom Pirandello's influence was most pervasive were thoroughly acquainted with his work. Thomas Bishop's study of the influence of Pirandello on the French theatre calls it 'certainly the most important foreign influence and very possibly the most important single influence of any kind' (p. 10). The performance of *Six Characters* by the Comédie des Champs-Elysées on 10 April 1923, in particular, had, in Bishop's words, 'the effect of an earthquake' (p. 5); since then, 'French plays depicting the relativity of truth, the multiplicity of personality, the art-life opposition, and the overwhelming absurdity of life have become familiar on the Parisian stage' (p. 146). 'Besides Pirandello,' he continues, 'only Shakespeare and Ibsen have left such a legacy and it is unlikely that either has affected the theater of a single country of any era more than the author of *Sei personaggi*. Of all the various forces that combined to mold the theatrical imagination of the French writers of our age, none was more widespread, none more penetrating, and none more productive than this' (pp. 147–8). Bishop quotes in support of his assertion a number of important French critics such as Brisson and Doisy (pp. 6, 9); Bernard Dort confirms that 'it is an unquestionable fact: Pirandello ... dominated the French theatre between the two wars and also during the immediate post-war period from 1945 to 1950 ... There is no French playwright of any consequence who is not in some way touched by Pirandello' (*Atti*, 51–2).

In France, Pirandellian themes first surfaced in the existentialist theatre of Sartre and Camus, and later in the Theatre of the Absurd. The 'sense of metaphysical anguish at the absurdity of the human condition,' which Martin Esslin traces from Sartre and Camus to Beckett, Adamov, Ionesco, Genet, and the other writers of the Theatre of the Absurd (p. xix), entered the existentialist theatre and fiction of Sartre and Camus by way of Pirandello, a debt that, curiously, Esslin totally ignores. Pirandello's Henry IV had suffered from an awareness of 'the absurdity of the human condition' with as much anguish as – and many years earlier than – Camus' Caligula and Mersault (*L'étranger*) and Sartre's Goetz (*Le Diable et le bon Dieu*). Again ignoring its source in Pirandello, Esslin finds the 'sense of the senselessness of life, of the inevitable devaluation of ideals, purity, and purpose,' precisely the feelings that we have recognized as one of the major reasons for the Pirandellian character's revolt, in Giraudoux, Anouilh, Salacrou, Sartre, and Camus, as well as in their successors, the playwrights of the Absurd (ibid.).

Tied to this 'devaluation of ideals' is 'the sense that the certitudes and unshakable basic assumptions of former ages have been swept away, that they had been tested and found wanting, that they have been discredited as cheap and somewhat childish illusions,' which is the 'hallmark,' in Esslin's words, 'of an age of transition' (p. xviii). And this too is a theme that came to the Theatre of the Absurd by way of the existentialists, but whose origin is clearly Pirandellian. For the age of Pirandello had been even more distinctly an 'age of transition'; the root of the drama of his characters had been the loss of the sense of stability, self-confidence, and unity, of the community of thought and belief that had been the hallmark of the bourgeois world of the end of the century. Esslin observes that for Camus, 'in a world of shattered beliefs ... life had lost all meaning ...; in a universe that is suddenly deprived of illusion and of light, man feels a stranger, he is an irremediable exile'; he quotes Ionesco to the effect that 'cut off from his religious, metaphysical roots, man is lost; all his actions become senseless, absurd, useless' (p. xix); but he seems unaware that both the existentialist writer and the dramatist of the Absurd are expressing ideas and feelings widely developed in Pirandello's work.

That sense of loss of 'the certitudes and unshakable basic assumptions of former ages' led in Pirandello first (*Mrs Morli, One and Two, Right You Are, if You Think You Are, Henry IV, Each in His Own Way*, etc.), and then in the existentialists and the Theatre of the Absurd, to the recurring theme of obsessive self-doubt and the quest for identity. Yet when he recognizes it in Beckett, Esslin chooses to trace it to Beckett's Irish Protestant origins (pp. 1–2) rather than to Pirandello. Uncertainty about one's identity is caused not only by the loss of earlier certitudes, but also by the sense of the change constantly occurring in our personality, its instability, as well as its complexity and multiplicity. And once again Esslin tells us that this concept is an original idea of Beckett who, in an early critical essay on Proust, had formulated it as an aspect of his interpretation of the French writer: 'Yesterday has deformed us ... yesterday is irremediably part of us, within us, heavy and dangerous. We are not merely weary because of yesterday, we are other, we are no longer what we were before the calamity of yesterday' (p. 17). But this sense of the fluidity of personality is very close to what the Father of *Six Characters* has expressed to the Director:

> Only to find out if you, as you are now, really see yourself as you now see, for instance, from a distance, what you once were, with all the illusions you had then? with all the things, inside and outside of you, the way they seemed to you – and were, really were for you? – Well, sir, thinking of all those illusions long gone, of all the things that no longer 'seem' to you the way they 'were' then, don't you feel ... the ground itself giving way under your feet, realizing that in the same way 'everything' you feel 'is' here and now, everything that is for you today, is bound to reveal itself an illusion tomorrow? (I 104)

Of the complexity and multiplicity of personality, Pirandello had written years before, in his essay *On Humor*:

> The many tendencies that distinguish the personality compel us to think seriously that the individual soul is not one. How indeed can it be considered *one*, if passion and reason, instinct and will, tendencies and ideals, make up in a way as many separate and mobile systems, which make it seem as if in the individual, who lives now one, now another of them, now some compromise between two or more psychic orientations, various dif-

ferent and even opposing souls, various opposing personalities, actually coexisted?[30]

The technique of splitting various aspects of a complex personality according to the different 'elements within a single personality, particularly if that personality is in conflict with itself,' which Esslin finds (p. 32) in various playwrights of the Theatre of the Absurd, had been very brilliantly employed by Pirandello, in *Six Characters*, for instance, where the Father and the Stepdaughter embody highly developed consciousness, the Mother embodies pure feeling, and the two speechless children an apparent lack of awareness. This technique of having different characters embody the different aspects of a single personality ('Pozzo and Lucky have been interpreted as body and mind ... Each of these pairs – Pozzo–Lucky, Vladimir–Estragon, Hamm–Clov – is linked by a relationship of mutual interdependence, wanting to leave each other, at war with each other, and yet dependent on each other,' p. 31) is also clearly related to the Pirandellian technique of 'role-playing,' in which the character chooses to play or is compelled to play different roles, wear different masks, lead different lives, as in *Mrs Morli, One and Two, As You Want Me, Right You Are, if You Think You Are, Role Playing* [*Il giuoco delle parti*], *Henry IV, Each in His Own Way*, and as Mattia Pascal decides to do in the various phases of his life. This typical Pirandellian game of role-playing reappears continually in the Theatre of the Absurd: Genet's two maids play the role of maid and madame on alternate days, and become so engrossed in the character they play that, one day, while playing madame, Claire actually drinks the poison intended for her employer; in Ionesco's *The Chairs*, the personalities of husband and wife change drastically with the arrival of their imaginary guests; Adamov's Professor Taranne, the university scholar who is highly thought of and must live up to his reputation by faking and stealing ideas from his colleague Menard, cannot endure the mask he has been wearing: he tears it off a little too drastically and is found walking naked in a city street.

As Pirandello's characters are assailed by doubts as to their identity, they are equally troubled about the possibility of ever establishing or communicating it through a normal, functioning relationship with the society they live in. The theme of the difficulty of communication and the inadequacy of language as a vehicle of communication is the central theme of the theatre of Pirandello's maturity (*Right You Are, Six Characters, The Mountain Giants*, etc.) as it is at the centre of many plays of the

Theatre of the Absurd (*Waiting for Godot*, *The Chairs*, etc.). Esslin quotes Beckett as saying: 'Art is the apotheosis of solitude. There is no communication because there are no vehicles of communication' (p. 4); and tells us that Ionesco 'protested against the imputation [by Tynan] that he ... maintained the impossibility of communication by language,' by replying that 'the very fact of writing and presenting plays is surely incompatible with such a view. I simply hold that it is difficult to make oneself understood' (p. 80). Following Ellmann, Esslin tells us that 'Beckett read Joyce passages from the work of Fritz Mouthner, whose *Critique of Language* was one of the first works to point to the fallibility of language for the discovery and communication of metaphysical truths' (p. 5). But Beckett, who, unlike Esslin, knew Pirandello, of course had read similar ideas in Pirandello's major works, such as *Six Characters* where the Father says:

But this is where the root of all evil lies! in words! We all have a world of things inside of us; each a world of his own! And how can we understand each other, sir, if in the words I use I put the meaning and value of things as they are within me; while those who listen inevitably invest my words with their own meaning and value from the world within themselves? We think we understand each other, but we never do! (I 65)

Many other aspects of the human predicament dramatized by Pirandello are central to the existentialist theatre and the Theatre of the Absurd. Suffering is man's fate, particularly if he is capable of thinking. In Pirandello the more man suffers the more he thinks:

Is it not perhaps true that man never reasons so passionately ... as when he is suffering, because he wants to see the roots of his suffering, he wants to know who caused it and whether it was justified, while when he is happy, he accepts his happiness without reasoning about it, as if it were his right? ('Postscript' to *The Late Mattia Pascal*)[31]

And if at times the characters of the Theatre of the Absurd try not to think, to escape suffering ('Vladimir and Estragon's pastimes are, as they repeatedly indicate, designed to stop them from thinking,' Esslin tells us [p. 25]; 'We are in no danger of thinking anymore' [ibid.], they say with relief), it is because for them too thinking and suffering are causally linked.

Another double-edged sword dangling over the existence of the characters of Pirandello, of Sartre and Camus, and of the Theatre of the Absurd, is that of illusions, often indistinguishable from reality. While illusions give their world an appearance of stability, they also conspire to push man into playing roles, wearing masks, depriving him of the absolute freedom he aspired to, as in *Les Sequestrés d'Altona*, according to Bernard Dort 'Sartre's most Pirandellian play' (*Atti*, pp. 67–8). As not thinking can help us escape the inevitability of suffering, so illusions can help us avoid facing the bitterness of reality: Estelle and Garcin of Sartre's *Huis Clos* feel so comfortable in the illusions they have created for themselves that the revelation of the truth about themselves consti-tutes their infernal punishment. Sartre often forces this revelation on his characters through the eminently Pirandellian device of the mirror. This stratagem is also used by Ionesco, who, among avant-garde play-wrights, Bernard Dort tells us, is 'unquestionably' the one to whose work 'we must look for the omnipresent traces of Pirandellism,' begin-ning with the 'traditional confusion between life and theatre' (*Atti*, p. 71), the relativity of reality, and the plurality of truth. These 'traces' are particularly visible in *Rhinocéros*, at the end of which Bérenger, the only character to remain human, confronts himself in a mirror. The notion of the 'rhinocerization' of humanity in the industrial age is itself probably derived from Pirandello's mountain giants and their dehumanized workers; the famous scene of the thronging rhinos in *Rhinocéros* may well have been suggested to Ionesco by the mountain giants' roaring cavalcade, which makes the villa of the Scalognati shake and casts ter-ror into all its inhabitants.

If Pirandello's influence on the existentialist writers and the Theatre of the Absurd has been so unpardonably ignored in some quarters, the debt owed Pirandello by the expressionist theatre has been widely acknowledged.[32] Less recognized, however,[33] is Bertolt Brecht's indebt-ness to Pirandello, which is at least as great as that of the existentialists and expressionists. Brecht became thoroughly acquainted with Piran-dello's work during the years of his literary apprenticeship, 1920 to 1930; a good number of Pirandello's plays were performed with great success in Germany,[34] and Brecht not only saw them, but had access to the texts, published in 1925 in translation in two volumes, and may even have assisted in staging some of them. Still, the majority of critics continue to credit Brecht's encounter with the Russian formalists and the performance of a Chinese theatrical troupe during a Moscow visit in 1935 for many influences that are more clearly Pirandellian and which are already discernible in *A Man's a Man* (1924–6), *The Threepenny*

Opera (1928), and *Saint Joan of the Stockyards* (1930), all written before the Moscow visit, not only in the works that came after it.

The theme of a relativistic perception of reality, including the perception of oneself and others, is already at the centre of *A Man's a Man*, together with the theme of the continuous evolution of both the human personality and the world surrounding it; the protagonist is made to undergo the drastic and deliberate changes, as do Henry IV or Mattia Pascal or the protagonists of *Each in His Own Way* or *One, No One, One Hundred Thousand*, to adapt to the reality around him, or to attempt to control it, or merely survive, changes as extreme as the total loss of personality in the definitive defeat and solitude of the useless survivor, as is the case with the late Mattia Pascal and Vitangelo Moscarda. Of course, the motif of the changing or splitting of personality will also appear in works following the Moscow period, from *The Good Woman of Setzuan* to *Mother Courage* to *Galileo*.

In both Pirandello and Brecht this relativism of the human perception of reality and its continuous transformations are at the root of the difficulty of human communication, of the loss of the absolute values of former ages and the stability they fostered in the individual, who today instead feels 'the ground giving way under his feet' before the perception of the continuous change of his inner reality and of the world around him.

Some familiar images of Brecht's iconography are more than likely of Pirandellian origin, such as the cart that Mother Courage and her children pull, which repeats the image of the Thespian cart of Pirandello's Ilse; so too are certain situations in *The Caucasian Chalk Circle*, such as the discussion about whether its owner or the person who works it has more right to the land, strongly recalling a spirited passage in *Liolà*, or the motif of the strength of the maternal feelings of the adoptive mother, which recurs in many of Pirandello's works, such as 'Scialle nero,' 'Pena di vivere cosí,' etc.

But most significantly, years before Brecht met the Russian formalists and particularly Sklovskij, he encountered in Pirandello the suggestion that art is not an imitation of the outer appearances of life; that the theatre should not hypnotize the spectator with the perfect illusion of reality, nor lull him into the distension of a catharsis or of a happy ending, but should keep alive in him till the end the tension that it arouses; that it should engage not only his feelings, but also his intelligence and his reflection (through the creation of an intellectual tension). Art, in Pirandello's words, is not the mirror of life, but ought to be a mirror *for* life, in the sense that life looking at itself would never be able to see what is revealed to it by the work of art, because the artist's eye can reach its essence, its most hidden truth, all that is 'less real, perhaps, but truer,' as Pirandello would say. And the modern artist should reveal the less obvious, less familiar reality he is capable of seeing, in a non-obvious, non-familiar manner, in an unusual context, in unexpected configurations, thus achieving what the Russian formalists were to call 'defacilitation' and 'defamiliarization,' in essence the 'estrangement' clearly present in Brecht's works well before the Moscow visit, particularly in *A Man's a Man*, the most Pirandellian of his plays.

Moreover, many of the well-known techniques employed by Brecht to achieve that 'estrangement' or 'distancing,' which prevents the spectator from becoming too emotionally involved in the character's drama, which challenges him continuously, were first used by Pirandello. A primary tactic is to keep reminding the spectator that he is facing not reality and real people but a created work, performed by actors, on a stage. To this end Pirandello and Brecht after him keep the stage machinery visible, begin the play with the rehearsal of another play, and use the technique of the play within the play in a new, more ambitious, more meaningful way. They may employ a kind of prologue (given to the Stepdaughter in *Six Characters*, for example, and to Doctor Hinkfuss in *Tonight We Improvise*) partly revealing the dramatic action to come, so that more attention will be directed to the meaning; they create characters who illustrate clearly, in both action and dialogue, the problems explored in the play – in *Right You Are, if You Think You Are*, for instance, the subjectivity of one's perception of reality is discussed directly, and in *A Man's a Man* the relativity of one's identity. Both permit an actor to step out of the role he is playing to address the audience directly; both create characters who act as the author's mouthpiece, and who clarify the action and the themes of the play for the audience (as the *raisonneur* of the grottesco theatre did, as Laudisi does in the most 'grottesco' of Pirandello's plays, or as Doctor Hinkfuss does in *Tonight We Improvise*), characters who act as bridges between the play and the spectator and compel him to bring his intelligence to bear on the dynamics of the play. Finally, both Pirandello and Brecht alter the traditional relationship between plot and character: they do away with the subordination of the character to the causal logic of events; the character becomes the embodiment of the author's vision of reality; the plot is liberated from linear chronological and causal development, and consequently from its rigid subdivision into acts and its conventional distribution of climactic moments, in favour of an at least apparently chaotic and unpredictable development.[35]

Not only in content, then, but in form as well – the theatrical innovations he created to dramatize the crisis of our time – Pirandello influenced the work of many Western novelists and playwrights from the twenties to the present. His use of the stage in particular was enormously influential: it broke through the strictures of time and space imposed by theatrical tradition, opened the stage space to unthought-of possibilities, and pointed the way the avant-garde was to take to expand our idea of the theatre. 'The striking modernity of his approach appealed to many French dramatists and the lessons Pirandello taught were taken seriously,' Bishop has observed (p. 146). It was from Pirandello that Ionesco, Beckett, Adamov, and Genet learned to use the theatre experimentally, to look for 'new, essentially dramatic expression,' to 'approach the play primarily as a function of the theater,' investigating 'every avenue of theatricality and invention that might extend the limits of the stage' (Bishop, p. 134). Guy Dumur asserted that 'one cannot come close to defining Pirandellism without taking into account the technical and aesthetic aspects of his vision of reality, which are those of a theatre that is new.'[36] Marcel Doisy's 1947 essay on contemporary French theatre concluded, 'Surely no man of the theatre since Ibsen had given Europe so totally renewed a concept of the theatre, a more violently original artistry together with so personal a technique ... and it certainly seems his revelations are still far from exhausted.'[37] Eugene Ionesco acknowledged his debt in the largest possible terms: 'Pirandello's theatre does, in fact, meet the ideal exigencies of the structures, of the dynamic architecture of the drama. It is the manifestation of the inalterable archetype of the idea of the theatre we have in us.'[38]

Pirandello's dramatic vision of the crisis of humanity in our time was a model, then, to which all his successors looked, and it continues to be the most powerful theatre we have, in part because it avoids the faults of his successors, their excessive simplifications, their frequent predictability, their exaggerated belabouring of already obvious themes. An example we might examine is Beckett's celebrated *Waiting for Godot*. Esslin informs us that its first London performance in 1955 'had met with a measure of incomprehension. Indeed the verdict of most critics was that it was *completely obscure, a farrago of pointless* chit-chat' (p. ix, 1969 ed.). He furnishes the obvious explanation that this phenomenon occurs whenever something radically new is presented to 'a public conditioned to an accepted convention'; it tends to receive the impact of artistic experience through a filter of critical standards, of predetermined expectations and terms of reference, which is the natural result of the schooling of his taste and faculty of perception. This framework of values, admirably efficient in itself, produces only bewildering results when it is faced with a completely new and revolutionary convention – a tug of war ensues between the impressions that have undoubtedly been received and critical perceptions that clearly exclude the possibility that any such impression could have been felt. Hence the storm of frustration and indignation always caused by works in a new convention. (pp. xxiii–xxiv)

This was, of course, precisely the response to Pirandello's most original plays, and particularly to the first performance of *Six Characters* at the Valle Theatre in Rome in 1921, on the part of a public accustomed for more than fifty years to the conventions of the bourgeois and naturalistic theatre. And, indeed, even today Pirandello's work still sometimes meets with a wide 'measure of incomprehension,' as we have seen in connection with the 1973 Broadway production of *Henry IV*.[39]

Esslin considers it a glorious vindication, which he reports with considerable irony, that while in 1955 *Waiting for Godot* had met with so much critical incomprehension, the 1964 performance 'was extremely favorably received by the critics. As to the play – the general verdict seemed that it was a modern classic now but had one great fault: its meaning and symbolism were a little too obvious' (p. ix, 1969 ed.). Esslin invites us to believe that if the critics were wrong in 1955 in saying that the play was 'completely obscure,' they must have been wrong in 1964 also, in saying that 'its meaning and symbolism were a little too obvious.' Yet today it is very difficult not to agree with both critical evaluations of the meaning and symbolism of *Waiting for Godot*: if the play did appear somewhat obscure at first, it also, on examination, now that the superficial novelty has worn off, seems lacking in complexity and depth.

With the passing of time, some of the work of Brecht too – with its exaggerations and simplifications, the all too obvious political arguments, the flattened characters – compares poorly with the complexity of Pirandello, the resistance of his characters to simple definition, the depth and richness of his plays. In the major works of Pirandello, as in all true classics, scholars continue to find new dimensions and new meanings; they continue to apply to them every possible critical approach, especially in these times of proliferating critical approaches;

artists continue to find in them inspiration and techniques to emulate.[40]

One reason for the durability of Pirandello, as compared with many of his successors, lies in the greater maturity with which he effected his revolution in the theatre. For a long time he worked almost exclusively within the pre-existing forms of the theatre of his time, before proposing radically new forms. These are the tactics of the most enduring literary revolutions, like that of Goldoni in transforming the form and content of the *commedia dell'arte*. When Pirandello approached his maturity as a writer, the Italian theatre had been dominated by one form of naturalism or another for half a century (much longer than had Italian fiction), by the 'verismo' theatre that dealt with the primitive conditions and customs of regional life, and especially by the 'bourgeois' theatre, as it has traditionally been called by Italian scholars, which dealt chiefly with the many aspects of the malaise of the urban bourgeoisie in a manner familiar in European drama from France and Germany to Russia and Scandinavia, a theatre always set in the bourgeois parlour, whose forms had become as conventional as its plots and situations, including the tendency towards an ending that satisfied, even when it was not 'literally' happy, the moral conventions of the time, often more concerned with the preservation of a façade of respectability than with the pursuit of truth. Pirandello's theatre, while it unmasks the pretentions to moral respectability, rationality, and stability and the behavioural conventions of the bourgeois world, also argues with the art forms that had celebrated them; but the earlier theatre of Pirandello does so by assuming those forms in order to denounce their incongruity. Instead of discarding them directly, from his first play on, Pirandello chooses first to present recognizable situations and types of the bourgeois world in order to demonstrate its alienating nature, and of the bourgeois theatre in order to unmask its sterile conventionality and demonstrate the need for new, open forms: if the tragedy of the character is insoluble, the new theatre must also shun the solutions dictated by the bourgeois theatre, particularly the deceptions of that third act, and transform its use of the traditional stage space.

Pirandello's theatre, that is, is already as revolutionary when it gives the impression of working within the conventions of the bourgeois theatre, as in *Right You Are, if You Think You Are*, as it is when it moves to entirely new ground, as in *Six Characters*. And *Six Characters* is revolutionary not merely because it proposes a totally new use of the scenic space, but – more importantly – because it proposed a totally new use of dramatic space and time, breaking through the limitations imposed on the theatre since time immemorial and altering the trajectory that the plot must follow. It is revolutionary not because it employs the technique of the play within the play (a familiar one even in the bourgeois theatre, as far back as Paolo Ferrari, though never used so radically), but because its characters consciously act as characters rather than persons, and because it succeeds in bringing to centre stage the nature and problems of artistic creation and expression, not only through witty, erudite exposition, but through the translation into powerful dramatic action of the existential themes of human communication, and of the need for and the difficulty of achieving a satisfactory integration of the individual in an alienating society. Finally, it is a revolutionary work in its multiple and complex structural and semantic levels. While the six characters believe that 'the drama that makes them dramatic characters and thanks to which they are dramatic characters' consists in the adventure of their family melodrama, and while they attempt to communicate it to the theatrical company, they unwittingly live out the real drama with which their creator has endowed them: the state of being in search of definitive artistic form; in the process the theatrical company, incapable of understanding and interpreting the new theatre of Pirandello at which it is trying its hand for the first time, is unwittingly drawn into a quintessentially Pirandellian play.

Not only does Pirandello approach his radical program gradually, he never yields, even in the most revolutionary of his plays, those that most poignantly dramatize 'the absurdity of the human condition,' to the temptation of formlessness and chaos. Esslin faults Sartre and Camus (and presumably would have faulted Pirandello as well) for continuing to express their 'sense of the irrationality of the human condition in the form of highly lucid and logically constructed reasoning,' and praises the Theatre of the Absurd enthusiastically because it 'strives to express its sense of the senselessness of the human condition and the inadequacy of the rational approach by the open abandonment of rational devices and discursive thought' (pp. xix–xx). In Esslin's view, 'Sartre and Camus express the new content in the old convention,' while 'the Theater of the Absurd goes a step further in trying to achieve a unity between its basic assumptions and the form in which they are expressed'; thus, he believes, 'in some sense the *theater* of Sartre and Camus is less adequate an expression of the *philosophy* of Sartre and Camus – in artistic, as distinct from philosophic terms – than the Theater of the Absurd' (p. xx). This seems to me a serious error of judgment. The idea that 'the irrationality of the human condition' cannot be adequately expressed in rational dramatic form is one of those absurd assumptions of immature minds out of which lasting works of art rarely arise. Pirandello had posed the question to himself and had arrived at a very different answer: 'I must express this organic and natural chaos; and expressing chaos does not at all mean expressing it in a chaotic manner' (I 45–6).

But the difference in form between Pirandello, Sartre, and Camus, on the one hand, and the playwrights of the Absurd on the other, is also due to a major difference in the reaction of the writers and their characters to the loss of 'the certitudes ... of former ages' (Esslin, p. xviii) and of their former sense of identity, and to the new feeling of the irrationality of the human condition. Confronting this traumatic discovery and perceiving that their destiny is irremediable, the characters of the Theatre of the Absurd seek solace in games that keep them from thinking, while the protagonists of Pirandello's theatre never cease to *reason* about its unfairness and absurdity. The Pirandellian characters do not merely intuit the irrationality of the human condition; they achieve a deep understanding of it, and thereby arrive at their definitive alienation, through a process that begins with a painful experience but is completed through persistent, impassioned reasoning, which, Pirandello maintains, is a natural activity of those who suffer ('man never reasons so passionately ... as when he is suffering').[41] Hence, for Pirandello the expression of suffering and the rational search for its explanation is a work of art fundamentally rational in its structure, and in the development of its events and their meanings – works, in short, whose artistic intention is to express the irrationality of life 'in the form of highly lucid and logically constructed reasoning,' through 'rational devices and discursive thought.'

If his mature approach to a revolution in the theatre is one explanation of Pirandello's enduring vitality and a modernity ultimately more profound than that of many of his successors, another, perhaps more important reason lies in his deeper understanding and more truthful representation of the spiritual and psychological crisis of man in our time. Many of the dramatists who came after Pirandello created characters who, having intuited the impossibility of attaining an unassailable reality and absolute truth and lamented its loss, have become resigned to the fall into formlessness, have delivered themselves to chaos and to definitive silence, depriving themselves of an essential human dimension. Instead, Pirandello's characters, while equally aware that they will never find a way out of the impasse, do not cease to search for one,

to proclaim their need for one, even to pursue unsatisfactory compromises, so strongly do they yearn for a reality that can be shared. They are
characters who do not accept, but suffer the loss of form and meaning,
and declare that loss an unjust privation, assert their need for that unity
and certainty as a fundamental and irrepressible human need, as an
inalienable right. The angry indictment of their loss, and the expression
of both the irrepressible need for what they have lost and the awareness
of the impossibility of recovering what they seek, is the existential contradiction, the drama they bring to the stage, which Pirandello calls the
drama of 'this formless life which yearns for form' (I 44).

While this traumatic discovery of irreparable loss would later afflict
the characters of the writers he influenced, it is that obstinate search
even when facing the impossible, the refusal to surrender to chaos, to
formlessness, to silence,[42] which distinguishes Pirandello's characters
from those of most subsequent theatre, and especially the Theatre of the
Absurd. Pirandello's is the most significant and profound expression of
the 'crisis of passage' from a nineteenth-century, bourgeois, positivist
culture to the irrationalist, relativistic culture of the new century, yet
he does not choose to cultivate – as various revolutionary and experimental currents of his time and thereafter did – a post-positivist irrationalism and nihilism; these he finds disturbing and deplorable. His
sensibility by preference always expressed bewilderment, compassion,
moral indignation, the irrepressible need to rebel; these in turn generate
the tension that makes his work an incomparably rich and vital reflection of the predicament of man in our time.

Notes

Chapter 1

1 Volume and page numbers throughout this book refer to the most authoritative edition of Luigi Pirandello's theatre, *Maschere nude*, 2 vols. (Milano: Mondadori, 1978). All translations from Pirandello in this book are my own.

2 Luigi Pirandello, *Saggi, poesie, scritti varii*, ed. Manlio Lo Vecchio Musti (Milano: Mondadori, 1960), p. 1246.

3 Pirandello's statement that 'in writing plays one does not imitate or copy "life," for the simple reason that there is no "life" that stands for "reality" as such, to be copied' (*Saggi*, p. 987) has led some scholars to think that Pirandello denies the existence of 'life' as distinct from 'art.' This is not the case. For Pirandello 'the illusions that we conceive about ourselves, others, and our surroundings' (in the words of one such scholar, Claudia Terzi, 'Le poetiche del grottesco,' in Luciano Anceschi, *L'idea del teatro e la crisi del naturalismo*, Bologna: Calderini, 1971, p. 74), that is, our 'perception of life,' may be *less true, perhaps, but more real* than its representation in 'art'; it *is* life – it is the root of a suffering that is real and not illusory. Art is not the root of that suffering; art is its expression. These scholars would do well to remember another statement of Pirandello: 'Life's absurdities don't have to seem believable, because they are real [*vere*]. As opposed to art's absurdities, which, to seem real [*vere*], have to be believable' (*The Late Mattia Pascal*, New York: Doubleday, 1966, p. 258). Here the distinction between 'art' and 'life' is clearly assumed, and 'reality' is seen as inherent in life, while the 'truth' of art is considered a hard-won achievement of the creative process.

4 *Saggi*, pp. 21–2.

5 Ibid., p. 24.

6 See, for example, Olga Ragusa, 'Correlated Terms in Pirandello's Concep-

tion of Umorismo,' *The Two Hesperias. Literary Studies in Honor of Joseph J. Fucilla on the Occasion of his 80th Birthday*, ed. Americo Bugliani (Madrid: Turanzas, 1978), p. 307.

7 Cf. *Saggi*, pp. 126–7.

8 See Ragusa, 'Correlated Terms,' p. 307.

9 Ruggero Jacobbi in 'Attualità ed inattualità di Pirandello,' in Sandro D'Amico, ed., *Pirandello ieri e oggi* (Milano: Quaderni del Piccolo Teatro, 1961), p. 26, excludes the existence of an epistemological component in favour of an exclusively ethical truth.

Chapter 2

1 One example is Michela Montante, 'Realism versus "Pirandellism" in *Liolà*,' *Forum Italicum*, 2, 17 (Fall 1983): 246–56, which states that Pirandello's art 'reflects the trends of "verismo"' (247); that *Liolà* is still tied to 'Capuana's theory of realism' (248), and 'belongs to the same ideological stream of literary-regional plays that have their beginning in Verga's *Cavalleria rusticana*, and a valuable illustration in Capuana's *Malía*' (255); that 'the characters of *Liolà* are the "real-to-life" peasants of the historical and social Girgenti countryside' (249); that 'here, Pirandello, like Verga in his mature works, reaches the "impersonality" of the realistic writer [249] . . . immerses the real-to-life Liolà in the historical environment of Sicily' (253); and finally that 'the desire of the characters to better their economical condition is the predominant theme of both Verga's *I Malavoglia* and Pirandello's *Liolà*' (250). All these statements very closely echo their source: Domenico Vittorini, *The Drama of Luigi Pirandello* (New York: Russell and Russell, 1969), which places many Pirandellian plays in the mainstream of naturalism (pp. 63–85) and singles out *Liolà* as the closest to Verga's work: 'The naturalistic theme in the particular and well-defined characters that naturalism assumed especially in Verga, Pirandello's great master, appears also in *Liolà*. The setting and the characters of this play share in a distinct manner the most salient traits of Verga's art. Liolà is a happy-go-lucky peasant, not different from Verga's primitive fishermen, with the difference that Verga reveals through his elementary and humble characters his thoughtful mind, brings into play a deep note of painful mirth before the contradictions of life' (p. 63); 'there is in the play an echo of the life that Verga depicted in *Cavalleria rusticana*. We find in both the same country setting, the same primitive people and passions. As in *Cavalleria* Lola and Santuzza are rivals, so are here Mita and Tuzza' (pp. 70–1).

2 *Almanacco Bompiani 1938* (Milano: Bompiani, 1938), p. 40.

3 Anne Paolucci, 'Theater of Illusion, Pirandello's *Liolà* and Machiavelli's *Mandragola*,' *Comparative Literature Studies*, 9, 1 (March 1972): 44–57.

4 However, the fact that Pirandello called *Liolà* 'commedia campestre,' a 'country comedy,' should not give rise to the type of futile discussion engaged in by Margaret Brose ('Structures of Ambiguities in Pirandello's *Liolà*,' *Yale Italian Studies*, 2, 2 [Spring 1978]: 116), who mistakes the meaning of the subtitle ('The generic label suggests that the play is a pastoral comedy'), and dedicates her essay to a thorough but misguided demonstration of how *Liolà* differs from 'pastoral drama.' But the 'ambiguities' are the author's own rather than Pirandello's. She first translates 'commedia campestre' as 'pastoral comedy,' and then discusses the play in relation to the conventions of 'pastoral drama.' Pirandello termed it 'commedia campestre,' not 'commedia pastorale,' let alone 'dramma pastorale,' simply because in his time 'commedia' was the generic term for any social drama (and in practice, therefore, would cover the bourgeois, the 'grottesco,' and the Pirandellian theatre), and because the action takes place in the country ('campestre'), not because it incorporates the chief elements of 'pastoral drama.'

5 *Short Stories by Luigi Pirandello* (New York: Simon & Schuster, [n.d., 4th paper printing]), pp. 224–50.

6 Luigi Pirandello, *The Late Mattia Pascal* (New York: Doubleday, 1966), p. 259.

7 Which might seem to be a logical corollary to the fact that in Pirandello 'man never reasons so passionately ... as when he is suffering,' because 'he wants to arrive at the root of his suffering' (ibid.), and that the more he thinks the more he suffers.

8 Some brother (since it seems to fall to brothers to defend or revenge the family's honour) surely would have done him in. Even in regard to Simone's treatment of Mita, Gesa says: 'If she had a brother at least! You can bet the old man wouldn't treat her that way – I assure you!' (II 653).

9 Thus, the evaluation of Margaret Brose, 'Structures of Ambiguities,' p. 116, that Liolà 'comprehends the ambiguous nature of reality and successfully manipulates it for an altruistic goal,' is true only if that 'altruism' is understood to be wholly relative. In a similar vein, Anne Paolucci calls the argument by which Liolà convinces Mita 'sincere and selfless' (*Pirandello's Theater*, Carbondale: Southern Illinois Univ. Press, 1974, p. 29).

10 Cosmo Crifò, *Il teatro di Pirandello dagli inizi a Enrico IV* (Palermo: Manfredi, 1979), p. 35; trans. mine.

11 Luigi Pirandello, *To Clothe the Naked and Two Other Plays*, trans. and ed. William Murray (New York: Dutton, 1962).

12 The plot may be schematized thus: 1. Liolà gets Tuzza pregnant, 2. Simone

assumes responsibility for her pregnancy, 3. Liolà gets Mita pregnant, 4. Simone claims responsibility for Mita's pregnancy and is persuaded that he should not deny his previously claimed responsibility for Tuzza's.

Liolà protagonist

Tuzza – deuteragonists – Mita

Simone antagonist

13 Some examples: s'accattu cchiú fruttu all'arbulu (II 646) = comprar frutta in erba (II 649); li picciotti nni sti discursi 'un si cci hannu a 'mmiscari (II 648) = questi non son discorsi in cui possono metter bocca le ragazze (II 651); haiu 'a chiurma all'antu e m'è jiri a guardari lu 'nteressu (II 732) = ho fuori le opere e voglio andare a badarle (II 733); ch'mmischeredda che si (II 654) = che ficchina (II 655); ma chi diavulu dici? (II 678) = stai farneticando (II 679); vitti ca sô figlia Tuzza cca' ... fici un saluni (II 678) = ho visto Tuzza springare un palmo da terra (II 679); stu bellu discursu (II 680) = codesto bel discorso (II 681); ha' la facci di veniri ccà (II 736) = hai la tracotanza di presentarti qua (II 737); ma taliati cu' parla di facci (II 736) = chi parla di tracotanza (II 737); c'appi lu curaggiu di diri (II 696) = ha avuto la tracotanza di dire (II 697); pu jucari (II 702) = cosí per ischerzo (II 703); quannu mi maritavu (II 708) = quando sposai (II 709); e a versu (II 728) = e fate con garbo (II 729); p'i coccia (II 728) = per piluccare qualche acinetto lasciato (II 729).

Chapter 3

1 'The Italian Director Face to Face with Pirandello,' *World Theater*, 16, 3 (May–June, 1967): 252.

Chapter 4

1 Luigi Pirandello, *Novelle per un anno*, vol. 1 (Milano: Mondadori, 1985), p. 816.
2 *Almanacco Bompiani 1938* (Milano: Bompiani, 1938), p. 43.
3 Beginning early in the century with the many 'discussion plays' by G.B. Shaw; see, for example, the dream sequence from the third act of *Man and Superman* (1901), often produced as a separate play, *Don Juan in Hell*.

4 Giambattista Vico, *Opere* (Milano: Ricciardi, 1953), p. 281; trans. mine.

Chapter 5

1 'Il teatro di Luigi Pirandello,' in *Studi sul teatro contemporaneo* (Roma, 1923), p. 183; trans. mine.
2 'Pirandellian Chinese Puzzle,' *New York Times* (29 March 1973): 42.
3 'We Are Utterly Unable to Leave *Henry* Alone,' *New York Times* (8 April 1973): 1. *Right You Are, if You Think You Are* as well as *It Is So, if You Think So* are common translations of the title of *Cosí è, se vi pare*.
4 Ibid., pp. 1, 16. The play has made a similar impression on other critics, whose work is perhaps less ephemeral than Kerr's, who are more familiar with Pirandello and at least equally well disposed towards him; see, for example, Frank L. Lucas, *The Drama of Chekhov, Synge, Yeats, and Pirandello* (London: Cassell, 1963), pp. 417–22; and in Italian, Roberto Alonge, 'La tragedia astratta dell'Enrico IV,' in *Il teatro di Pirandello. Convegno di studi* (Asti: Centro Nazionale di Studi Alfieriani, 1964), pp. 29–45.
5 Orazio Costa, '*Six Characters*, *Right You Are* and *Henry IV*,' World Theater, 16, 3 (May–June 1967): 252.
6 Ibid.
7 Tilgher, 'Il teatro di Luigi Pirandello,' pp. 183–4.

Chapter 6

1 Eugenio Levi, *Il lettore inquieto* (Milano: Il Saggiatore, 1964), p. 279.
2 Luigi Pirandello, *Saggi, poesie, scritti varii*, ed. Manlio Lo Vecchio Musti (Milano: Mondadori, 1977), p. 152.
3 Ibid., pp. 150–1.

Chapter 7

1 It is unfortunate that Robert Brustein (*The Theater of Revolt*, Boston: Little, Brown, 1964) bases his view of the essence of Pirandello's poetics ('[Pirandello] tells us, whatever is fixed in form is really dead,' p. 303) on these words, which the playwright puts in Hinkfuss's mouth with ironic intent. Brustein forgets that when in *Six Characters* the Father says, 'He who has the good fortune to be born a live character ... will never die! ... Who was Sancho Panza? Who was Don Abbondio? Yet they live forever because ... they had the good fortune to find ... an imagination that was able to ... make them live forever!' (I 58–9), the context is *not* ironic. Hence his interpretation of the

themes and meanings of the theatre trilogy is extremely narrow (pp. 309–16), and some of his views of other Pirandellian masterpieces are altogether wrong; for example, '*It Is So! (If You Think So)* is a fairly conventional exercise in the mode of the grotesque,' pp. 295–6). He also reaches the conclusion that Pirandello's art negates human life ('Like his philosophy, his art is a negation of life,' p. 303), failing to see it as a bitter condemnation of the way both the individual and society choose to live life.

2 *Petrarca fra Abelardo ed Eloisa ed altri saggi di letteratura italiana* (Bari: Adriatica, 1969), p. 247; trans. mine.

3 Guglielminetti's interpretive line was also taken by Roberto Alonge, *Pirandello tra realismo e mistificazione* (Napoli: Guida, 1972), and Giovanna Tomasello, 'La donna ne *La nuova colonia*,' in VV.AA., *La donna in Pirandello* (Agrigento: Centro Nazionale di Studi Pirandelliani, 1988), pp. 57–63. Perhaps it was the conclusion of the novel *L'isola felice* by the writer Silvia Roncella, the protagonist of Pirandello's novel, *Suo marito* (1911), which led these critics to talk about La Spera of *The New Colony* as a mother who generates and devours her own children whom she cannot relinquish. At the end of *L'isola felice*, the mother suffocates her child with a powerful embrace when it is being taken from her, and the earthquake takes place as a reaction by Nature horrified at such a crime. The fact that in *The New Colony* the earthquake is not the expression of Nature's horror at the mother's crime, but Nature's intervention to save La Spera and her son, constitutes a radical change that has taken place in La Spera's story – and in its meaning – in the intervening twenty-odd years. An initially more accurate reading of La Spera's 'motherly love' can be found in Mauro Buccheri, 'Pirandello oltre il nichilismo: il ritorno alla Madre come rigenerazione ne *La nuova colonia*,' in Ada Testaferri, ed., *Donna: Women in Italian Culture* (Toronto: Dovehouse Editions, 1989), pp. 305–16; but Buccheri then finds the new ideal of conduct for La Spera in none other than Liolà.

4 Quoting Mittner's *L'Espressionismo* (Bari: Laterza, 1965), pp. 102–3.

5 Vol. 2 (Milano: Garzanti, 1960), p. 338.

6 Giorgio Strehler, '*The Mountain Giants*,' *World Theater*, 16, 3 (May–June 1967): 264.

Chapter 8

1 Nevertheless, Martin Esslin's widely known *The Theater of the Absurd* (New York: Anchor Books, 1961) [hereafter simply Esslin in the text] mentions Pirandello only incidentally, noting, for example, that Ionesco 'considers Pirandello outdated' (p. 139; cf. also Beatrice Corrigan, 'Pirandello and the

Theater of the Absurd,' *Cesare Barbieri Courier*, 8, 1 [1961]: 3), or quoting without further comment a statement by Anouilh who describes the opening night of *Waiting for Godot* at the Théâtre de Babylone 'as equal in importance to the first performance of a Pirandello play by Pitoeff, in 1923' (p. 10). Esslin later tried to make amends for the unpardonable omission by including a chapter on Pirandello ('Pirandello: Master of the Naked Masks') in his *Reflections: Essays on Modern Theater* (New York: Doubleday, 1969), which shows a knowledge of Pirandello limited to the five plays included in *Naked Masks* (New York: Dutton, 1954).

2 Cf. the widely quoted statement by French playwright George Nuveau: 'Sans Pirandello ... nous n'aurions eu ni Salacrou, ni Anouilh, ni aujourd'hui Ionesco, ni ... mais je m'arrête, cette énumération serait interminable. Tout le théâtre d'une époque est sorti de cette piece (le *Six personnages en quète d'auteur*),' *Arts*, 602 (6–12 Jan. 1957): 2; quoted by Bernard Dort, 'Pirandello et la dramaturgie française contemporaine,' *Atti del Congresso Internazionale di Studi Pirandelliani* (Firenze: Le Monnier, 1967), p. 52 [hereafter simply *Atti* in the text]; and by Thomas Bishop, *Pirandello and the French Theater* (New York: NYU Press, 1960), p. 147 [hereafter simply Bishop in the text].

3 Numerous characters obviously nourished by D'Annunzio's rhetoric and his exaltation of the D'Annunzian superman, and shocked back to the painful reality of their everyday world, populate dozens of major and minor novels of that period, from the Alfonso Nitti of Svevo's *Una Vita* (1984) to Borgese's *Rubè* (1920).

4 Cf. Wilma Newberry, *The Pirandellian Mode in Spanish Literature from Cervantes to Sastre* (Albany: State Univ. Press of New York, 1973); Moses M. Nagy, 'A Quest for Truth through Love and Reason: Marivaux and Pirandello,' *Review of National Literatures*, 14 (1987): 47–57; Maria Valentini, *Shakespeare e Pirandello* (Roma: Bulzoni, 1990); Franco Zangrilli, *Pirandello e i classici, da Euripide a Verga* (Firenze: Cadmo, 1995) and *Le sorprese dell'intertestualità, Cervantes e Pirandello* (Torino: S.E.I., 1996).

5 See Miguel de Unamuno, 'Pirandello y yo,' *La nación* (Buenos Aires, 15 July 1953), in Antonio Illiano, *Introduzione alla critica pirandelliana* (Verona: Fiorini, 1976), pp. 183–6; 'Io e Pirandello,' *La fiera letteraria*, 19, 23 (June 1964): 3. See also: Frank Sedwick, 'Unamuno and Pirandello Revisited,' *Italica*, 33, 1 (March 1956): 40–51; Annamaria Kelly, *Il rapporto tra Unamuno e Pirandello nella critica letteraria contemporanea* (Palermo: Flaccovio, 1976).

6 Claudio Vicentini, 'Il problema del teatro nell'opera di Pirandello,' *Pirandello e il teatro del suo tempo*, ed. Stefano Milioto (Agrigento: Centro Nazionale di Studi Pirandelliani, 1983), pp. 9–19.

7 The most persistent among them is surely Mario Verdone, whose latest

attempt to link Pirandello to futurism seems to be 'Pirandello e il teatro sintetico,' in *Pirandello e il teatro del suo tempo*, ibid., pp. 65–72. For Verdone's full
thesis, however, see *Teatro del tempo futurista* (Roma: Lerici, 1969), especially
the chapter 'Il teatro sintetico futurista e le sue correnti,' pp. 83ff., where,
taking his lead as always from the futurist manifestos calling for a theatre
that is 'grotesque and eccentric ... absurd ... occultistic and magic ... abstract
... visionary ... ideological and polemical,' he ropes together as mere 'currents' of the 'teatro futurista sintetico' all the theatrical currents of the twentieth century that might exhibit even one of those characteristics.

8 As when his *Salamandra*, 'A Mythical Dream by Luigi Pirandello for a Dance
in Five Episodes by Massimo Bontempelli,' was performed together with
eleven pantomimes by other writers on 6 and 7 March 1928 in Turin, and on
21 March in Milan by the company of the Teatro della Pantomima Futurista
directed by Enrico Prampolini; the contemporary reviews of these performances appear in Giovanni Antonucci, *Cronache del teatro futurista* (Roma:
Edizioni Abete, 1975), pp. 247–54 [hereafter simply Antonucci in the text],
and Pirandello's text in *Saggi, poesie, scritti varii*, ed. Manlio Lo Vecchio
Musti (Milano: Mondadori, 1960), pp. 1185–90. See also Verdone, *Teatro del
tempo futurista*, p. 282, and Lia Lapini, *Teatro futurista italiano* (Milano: Mursia, 1977), p. 81, n. 18.

9 'Zang Tumb Tumb,' *Opere di F.T. Marinetti, 2, Teoria e invenzione futurista*, ed.
Luciano De Maria (Milano: Mondadori, 1968), p. 262.

10 Silvio D'Amico's review of the opening night of *Simultanina* at the Teatro
Argentina in Rome (*La tribuna* [Rome], 16 June 1931) begins: 'By now these
futurist evenings are no longer oriented to the future but to the past. In 1931
they continue to take place imperturbably in a 1911 atmosphere; they remind us of when, not long out of our teens, some of us were arguing whether
or not Marinetti was a revolutionary. Marinetti is still arguing as if it were
still 1911' (Antonucci, p. 287); trans. mine.

11 Surveys of futurist paintings can be found in Joshua C. Taylor, *Futurism*
(New York: Museum of Modern Art, 1961); Raffaele Carrieri, *Futurism* (Milano: Edizioni del Milione, 1963); Drudi Gambillo and Teresa Fiori, *Archivi
del Futurismo*, 2 vols. (Roma: De Luca, 1958); Maurizio Calvesi, 'Dinamismo
e simultaneità nella poetica futurista,' *L'arte moderna*, 5, *Il futurismo* (Milano:
Fabbri, 1967).

12 The texts of the manifestos can be found in Carrieri, *Futurism*; Gambillo and
Fiori, *Archivi del Futurismo*; Lapini, *Teatro futurista italiano*; and De Maria, ed.,
Opere di F.T. Marinetti. See also L. Scrivio, *Sintesi del futurismo. Storia e docu-
menti* (Roma: Bulzoni, 1968).

13 At least seventeen are collected in Lapini, *Teatro futurista italiano*, in about
fifty pages (97–145).

14 Only later was this play also staged, together with Marinetti's *Bianca e Rosso*, by Bragaglia (Antonucci, pp. 178–80).

15 Leonardo Bragaglia, *Interpreti pirandelliani (1910–1969)* (Roma: Trevi, 1969), p. 181.

16 See in this regard Alberto Cesare Alberti, *Il teatro nel fascismo: Pirandello e Bragaglia* (Roma: Bulzoni, 1974), which deals exclusively with Pirandello's brief tenure in the Teatro d'Arte. As its artistic director Pirandello even directed, on 31 March 1926, a play by Marinetti, *Vulcano* (Antonucci, pp. 211, 299), the reviews of which by Arnaldo Frateili (*Fiera letteraria*, [Roma] 2, 15 [11 April 1926]), Marco Ramperti (*L'Ambrosiano*, [Milano] 14 April 1926), and others can be consulted in Antonucci, pp. 213–22.

17 Verdone, *Teatro del tempo futurista*, pp. 337–8.

18 This is perhaps the least convincing of the inventions of futurist painting, as employed, for instance, by Balla's 'Dynamism of a Dog on a Leash,' 'Girl Running on a Balcony,' and 'Flight of Swallows'; the technique is derived from such primitive kinetographs as Muybridge's 'Zoogyroscope' or Edison's 'kinetograph' and 'kinetoscope.' See also the first twenty photographs in Anton Giulio Bragaglia's *Fotodinamismo futurista* (Torino: Einaudi, 1970) as well as those reproduced in Carrieri, *Futurism*, which are simply protracted exposures of moving objects, or multiple exposures. Other futurist painters, and Balla himself on other occasions, expressed powerful and impetuous movement without the use of multiple images, as in Boccioni's 'The City Rises,' 'Revolt in the Galleria,' 'States of mind,' etc., or in Carrà's 'Funerals of the Anarchist Galli,' etc.; an excellent selection can be seen in Taylor, Carrieri, Gambillo and Fiori, and Calvesi (note 11).

19 In his eagerness to seize yet another opportunity to proclaim Pirandello's literary indebtedness to himself, Marinetti commits a bad error of interpretation of this passage, which he quotes more amply than we have done: 'Romagnoli,' he says, 'is referring here to my simultaneous play of objects [dramma simultaneo di oggetti], *Vengono*, which suggested to Pirandello the entrance or apparition of the modiste Madame Pace in the second act of *Six Characters*, an entrance imposed by the presence of the coat-racks laden with hats' (De Maria, ed., *Opere di F.T. Marinetti*, p. cxx). But the apparition has nothing to do with the simultaneity Romagnoli was talking about, and is instead, as Verdone (*Teatro del tempo futurista*, p. 359) points out, an example of the magic, evocative power of the word. (Manfredi Piccolomini too, 'Sull'episodio di Madama Pace nei *Sei personaggi* di Pirandello,' *Rivista di Studi Italiani*, 3, 1 [June 1985]: 79–88, has been deceived by Marinetti's statement, and calls the apparition of Madame Pace an example of simultaneity.) Nor, of course, is the coming to life of the stuffed dolls in *The Mountain Giants*, mentioned by Verdone ('Pirandello e il teatro sintetico,' p. 68) as one

of the 'elements' that 'are common to both Pirandello and the futurists,' an instance of simultaneity. Elsewhere Verdone (*Teatro del tempo futurista*, p. 137) observes of these dolls that they might have been suggested to Pirandello by the 'recurring theme of the "mechanical doll" of the German and French romantics, and the robots of Villiers de l'Isle-Adam and Jarry,' through Marinetti's *Pompées électriques, Elettricità sessuale*, and *Roi Bombance*. This is possible, as long as we keep in mind that the coming to life of Pirandello's dolls is a brief episode that neither constitutes the central action nor expresses the major theme of *The Mountain Giants*, while the motif of the mannequin is at the centre of the plays mentioned by Verdone; we should also note that Pirandello knew those French and German authors as well as he knew Marinetti.

With respect to the futurists' claim to have begotten all of twentieth-century theatre including Pirandello, see also the 1920 *Documento 9: Il nuovo teatro italiano*, in Lapini, *Teatro futurista italiano*, p. 126.

In the article cited above Romagnoli had gone on to an even less defensible judgment: 'The influence of futurism was particularly visible in *Each in His Own Way*, an antipsychological and daring play' (Antonucci, p. 190), an absurdity matched by this of Marinetti: '*Six Characters in Search of an Author* by Pirandello contains, besides long, boring philosophical and psychological discussions of the most passé sort, some typically futurist scenes with objects that come to life' (De Maria, ed., *Opere di F.T. Marinetti*, 2, p. 146); trans. mine.

20 The three reviews collected by Antonucci, by Silvio d'Amico for *La tribuna* (Rome, 16 June 1931), by Eugenio Giovanetti for *Comoedia*, 13, 6 (Milan: 15 June–15 July 1931), by Mario Ferrigni for *L'illustrazione italiana*, 58, 20 (Milan: 17 May 1931), range from subtle irony to open sarcasm, although the three authors are Marinetti sympathizers.

21 For example, Douglass Radcliff-Umstead, *The Mirror of Our Anguish. A Study of Luigi Pirandello's Narrative Writings* (Cranbury, NJ: Associated University Presses, 1978), p. 130.

22 For example, Umberto Cantoro, *Luigi Pirandello e il problema della personalità* (Bologna: Gallo, 1954); Guido Favati, 'In margine all'*Étranger* di Camus: coincidenze con Luigi Pirandello,' *Rivista di letterature moderne e comparate*, 17, 2 (1984): 113–49; Hoover M. Clark, 'Existentialism in the *Sei personaggi*,' *Italica*, 43, 3 (Sept. 1966): 276–84; Vera Passeri Pignoni, 'Luigi Pirandello e la filosofia esistenziale,' *Atti*, 853–62; Madeleine Cincotta, 'L'esistenzialismo nelle novelle di Pirandello,' *Le novelle di Pirandello: Atti del Sesto Convegno Internazionale di Studi Pirandelliani* (Agrigento: Centro Nazionale di Studi Pirandelliani, 1980), pp. 103–17; idem, 'Existentialist Freedom in Luigi

Pirandello,' *Italian Quarterly,* 22, 86 (Fall 1981): 57–67; William Leparulo,
'Luigi Pirandello e Albert Camus,' *L'Italia nell'opera di Albert Camus* (Pisa:
Giardini, 1975), pp. 147–93; idem, 'Ipotesi per la risoluzione del rapporto
Pirandello-Camus,' *Italica,* 57, 1 (Spring 1980): 34–42; idem, 'Il teatro di Luigi
Pirandello e Albert Camus,' *Italian Quarterly,* 21, 80 (Spring 1980): 53–9;
Franca Angelini, 'Pirandello e Sartre,' *Pirandello e la cultura del suo tempo,* ed.
S. Milioto and E. Scrivano (Milano: Mursia, 1984), pp. 273–84; Vladimir
Krysinsky, 'Sartre et la métamorphose du cercle pirandellien,' *Sartre et la
mise en signe* (Lexington, KY: French Forum, 1982), pp. 83–102; Vincenzo
Chieppa, *Pirandello e Sartre* (Firenze: Kursaal, 1967); Joseph Venturini,
'Pirandello et les ideologies d'aujourd'hui,' *La nouvelle critique. Revue de
Marxism militant,* 233 (1972): 14–18.
23 Gaetano Munafò, *Conoscere Pirandello* (Firenze: Le Monnier, 1971), p. 269.
24 Ugo Spirito, *La vita come ricerca* (Firenze: Sansoni, 1943), pp. 104–5.
25 Ibid., p. 7.
26 Ibid., p. 8.
27 Ugo Spirito, *L'avvenire dei giovani* (Firenze: Sansoni, 1972), pp. 79–80.
28 Cf. note 22 above, as well as Gabriel Marcel, *Il problema del pirandellismo*
    (Padova: Cedam, 1984).
29 Anna Laura Lepschy, 'La presenza di Pirandello in Tom Stoppard,' *Piran-
    dello: poetica e presenza,* ed. W. Geerts, F. Musarra, and S. Vanvolsen (Roma:
    Bulzoni, 1987), pp. 453–65. And see also Luigi Baldacci, 'Il teatro di Bontem-
    pelli e l'esempio di Pirandello,' *Paragone,* 12, 144 (Dec. 1961): 25–34; Richard
    A. Sogliuzzo, 'The Use of the Mask in *The Great God Brown* and *Six Characters
    in Search of an Author,*' *Educational Theater Journal,* 18 (1966): 224–9; Sandro
    Sticca, 'The Drama of Being and Seeming in Schnitzler's *Anatol* and Piran-
    dello's *Cosí è, se vi pare,*' *Journal of the International Arthur Schnitzler Research
    Association,* 5, 51 (1966): 4–28; Federico Doglio, 'Pirandello e il nuovo teatro,'
    Studium, 63 (1967): 585–95; Bredrick Baumann, 'George H. Mead and Luigi
    Pirandello: Some Parallels between Theoretical and Artistic Presentation of
    the Social Role Concept,' *Social Research,* 34, 3 (1967): 563–607; William E.
    Taylor, '*Six Characters in Search of an Author* and *Desire under the Elms*: What
    O'Neill Did Not Learn from Europe,' in *Modern American Drama: Essays in
    Criticism,* ed. William E. Taylor (Leland, FL: Everett Edwards, 1969); Erminio
    Giuseppe Neglia, *Pirandello y la dramatica Rioplatense* (Firenze: Valmartina,
    1970); Rita Molfitano Verdirame, 'Pirandello e Brancati,' *Le ragioni critiche,* 2,
    4 (April–June 1972): 235–41; Vladimir Krysinsky, 'Pirandello et Gombrow-
    icz, deux visions de l'homme inauthentique,' *Rivista di letterature moderne e
    comparate,* 26 (1973): 173–96; Richard Gilman, *The Making of Modern Drama*
    (New York: Farrar Straus, 1974); Federico Frascani, 'L'incontro con Piran-

dello,' in *Eduardo* (Napoli: 1974); Sabato Magaldi, *O cenario no avesso: Gide e Pirandello* (São Paulo: Editora Perspectiva, 1977); D. De Camillis, 'Per un parallelo possibile: Cesare Pavese e Luigi Pirandello,' *Studi meridionali offerti a Aldo Vallone*, 2nd tome (Firenze: Olschki, 1987), pp. 561–74; Mary T. Reynolds, 'Joyce e Pirandello,' *Review of National Literatures*, 14 (New York: Griffon House, 1987): 58–78; Giancarlo Mazzacurati, *Pirandello e il romanzo europeo* (Bologna: Il Mulino, 1987); Gavriel Moses, '"Speculation" on Pirandello and Nabokov on "Specularity,"' *Pirandello '86*, ed. G.P. Biasin and N.J. Perella (Roma: Bulzoni, 1987), pp. 135–48; G.P. Biasin, 'From Shanghai to Cairo: Pirandellian Palimpsests,' ibid., 31–44, or 'Da Shanghai al Cairo: Palinsesti pirandelliani,' in *Pirandello: poetica e presenza*, pp. 33–46; Franco Zangrilli, *Linea pirandelliana nella narrativa contemporanea* (Ravenna: Longo, 1990, containing essays on the influence of Pirandello on Calvino, Sciascia, Bonaviri, Pomilio, Pontiggia, Altomonte); Godwin O. Uwah, *Pirandellism and the Plays of Samuel Beckett* (Potomac, MD: Scripta Humanistica, 1991). All translations from French and Italian quotations in this chapter are mine.
30 Pirandello, *Saggi*, p. 150. Cf. also Luigi Pirandello, *On Humor*, trans. A. Illiano and D.P. Testa (Chapel Hill: Univ. of North Carolina Press, 1974), p. 136.
31 Luigi Pirandello, *Il fu Mattia Pascal* (Milano: Mondadori, 1971), p. 253; cf. also *The Late Mattia Pascal*, trans. William Weaver (New York: Doubleday, 1966), p. 259.
32 See, for example, Oscar Budel, 'Contemporary Theater and Aesthetic Distance,' *PMLA*, 76, 3 (1961): 281–2; Gabriella Corsinovi, *Pirandello e l'espressionismo: analogie culturali e anticipazioni* (Genova: Tilgher, 1979).
33 See G.H. McWilliam, 'Interpreting Betti,' *Tulane Drama Review*, 5, 2 (1960): 17; and Antonio Illiano, *Introduzione alla critica pirandelliana* (Verona: Fiorini, 1976), p. 178, for the question as to whether Pirandello did or did not influence Brecht; and the entire chapter, 'Pirandello e ...,' about the relationship between Pirandello and other European literatures, particularly Spanish.
34 A list of them is given in Mario Mignone, 'The Theater of Pirandello and Brecht: Some Points of Contact,' *NEMLA Italian Studies*, 2 (1978): 64–5.
35 Pirandello's ideas on this point are clearly stated in *L'umorismo*, in *Saggi*, pp. 133ff. Cf. also Pirandello, *On Humor*, pp. 119ff.
36 *Le théâtre de Pirandello* (Paris: L'Arche, 1967), p. 11.
37 *Le théâtre français contemporain* (Brussels: La Beotie, 1947), p. 272.
38 'Pirandello vous a-t-il influencé?' *Arts*, 602 (16–22 Jan. 1957): 2.
39 At the beginning of ch. 5.
40 Manuela Gieri, *Contemporary Italian Filmmaking. Strategies of Subversion. Pirandello, Fellini, Scola, and the Directors of the New Generation* (Toronto: Univ.

of Toronto Press, 1995) shows the enormous influence of Pirandello on some of the major film-makers of our time.

41 Pirandello, *Il fu Mattia Pascal*, p. 253.

42 In a very interesting chapter of *The Drowned and the Saved* (New York: Simon & Schuster, 1988) on 'Communicating,' Primo Levi agrees with Pirandello that communication is a fundamental and irrepressible human need: 'To refuse to communicate is a failing; we are biologically and socially predisposed to communication, and in particular to its highly evolved and noble form, which is language' (p. 89).

Selected Bibliography

In English

Works of Pirandello

THEORETICAL WRITINGS

On Humor. Intro. and Trans. Antonio Illiano and Daniel P. Testa. Chapel Hill: Univ. of North Carolina Press, 1974.
'Theater and Literature,' trans. A.M. Webb; 'The New Theater and the Old,' trans. Herbert Goldstone, in *The Creative Vision. Modern European Writers on Their Art.* Ed. Haskell M. Blok and Herman Saliger. New York: Grove Press; London: Evergreen Books, 1960.

THEATRE

As You Desire Me. Trans. Samuel Putnam. New York: Dutton, 1931; trans. Marta Abba. New York: Samuel French, [1959]; trans. Marta Abba, in J. Gassner, ed. *Twenty Best European Plays on the American Stage.* New York: Crown, 1957.
Diana and Tuda. Trans. Marta Abba. New York: Samuel French, [1960].
'Dream, But Perhaps Not.' Trans. S. Putnam. *This Quarter* (June 1930).
'Doctor's Duty.' Trans. O.W. Evans. *Poet Lore* (1942): 291–304.
Each in His Own Way and Two Other Plays. Trans. A. Livingston. New York: Dutton; London: Dent, 1924. [*The Pleasure of Honesty, Naked*].
The Emperor. Trans. Eric Bentley, in *The Genius of the Italian Theater.* New York: Mentor, 1964.
'The Festival of Our Lord of the Ship.' In M. McKlintock, ed. *The Nobel Prize Treasury.* Garden City, NY: Doubleday, 1948.
To Find Oneself. Trans. Marta Abba. New York: Samuel French, [1959].

Henry IV. Trans. Edward Storer, in B. Ulanov, ed. *Makers of the Modern Theater.* New York: McGraw Hill, 1961.

Lazarus. Trans. Phillis H. Raymond. Sydney: Dante Alighieri, 1952.

Limes from Sicily and Other Plays. Trans. Robert Rietti. Leeds: S.J. Arnold, 1967.

'The Man with the Flower in His Mouth.' Trans. Eric Bentley. *Tulane Drama Review,* 1, 3 (June 1957): 15–22. Trans. F. May, *New Troy,* 1, 1 (June 1957).

The Mountain Giants and Other Plays. Trans. Marta Abba. New York: Crown, 1958. [*The New Colony, When Someone is Somebody*].

Naked Masks. Ed. Eric Bentley. New York: Dutton, 1952, 1958. [*Liolà,* trans. Eric Bentley and G. Guerrieri; *It Is So (If You Think So),* trans. A. Livingston; *Henry IV,* trans. E. Storer; *Six Characters,* trans. E. Storer; *Each in His Own Way,* trans. A. Livingston].

No One Knows How. Trans. Marta Abba. New York: Samuel French, [1961].

The One Act Plays of Luigi Pirandello. New York: Dutton, 1928. ['Chee-Chee,' 'Sicilian Limes,' 'By Judgment of the Court,' 'The Vise,' 'The House with the Column,' trans. Elizabeth Abbott; 'At the Gate,' 'The Imbecile,' 'Our Lord of the Ship,' 'The Doctor's Duty,' trans. Blanche Valentine Mitchell; 'The Jar,' 'The Man with the Flower in His Mouth,' trans. Arthur Livingston].

Pirandello's Major Plays. Trans. Eric Bentley. Evanston, IL: Northwestern Univ. Press, 1991. [*Right You Are, Six Characters, Emperor Henry, The Man with the Flower in His Mouth*].

Pirandello's One Act Plays. Trans. William Murray. Garden City, NY: Doubleday, 1964. ['Bellavita,' 'Cecè,' 'I'm Dreaming, But Am I?,' 'The Jar'].

Pirandello's One Act Plays. New York: Funk and Wagnalls, 1970. ['The Vise,' 'Sicilian Limes,' 'The Doctor's Duty,' 'The Jar,' 'The License,' 'Chee-Chee,' 'At the Exit,' 'The Imbecile,' 'The Man with the Flower in His Mouth,' 'The Other Son,' 'The Festival of Our Lord of the Ship,' 'Bellavita,' 'I'm Dreaming, But Am I?'].

'The Rest is Silence.' Trans. Frederick May. Leeds: The Pirandello Society, 1958.

Right You Are. A stage version. Trans. Eric Bentley. New York: Columbia Univ. Press, 1954.

Right You Are! (If You Think So). Trans. Henry Reed. Harmondsworth: Penguin, 1962. [*All for the Best*].

'Sicilian Limes.' Trans. Isaac Goldberg, in *Plays of the Italian Theater.* Boston: J.W. Luce, 1921; in *Theater Arts Magazine,* 6, 4 (1922).

Six Characters in Search of an Author. Trans. Edward Storer, in J. Gassner, ed. *A Treasury of the Theater,* 2. New York: Simon & Schuster, 1951.

Six Characters in Search of an Author. Trans. Frederick May. London: Heinemann, 1954, 1958.

Six Characters in Search of an Author. Adapt. Paul Avila Mayer, in R.W. Corrigan, ed. *Masterpieces of the Modern Italian Theater.* New York: Collier, 1967.

Six Characters in Search of an Author, The Emperor. Trans. Eric Bentley, in Robert Corrigan, ed. *The Modern Theater.* New York: MacMillan, 1964, 1965.

Three Plays. New York: Dutton, 1922, 1932; London: Dent, 1923, 1925, 1929. [*Six Characters, Henry IV,* trans. Edward Storer; *Right You Are,* trans. Arthur Livingston].

Three Plays. Harmondsworth: Penguin, 1959. [*The Rules of the Game,* trans. R. Rietty; *The Life I Gave You, Lazarus,* trans. Frederick May].

Three Plays. Harmondsworth: Penguin, 1960. [*Henry IV, Right You Are (If You Think So),* trans. Frederick May; *All for the Best,* trans. Henry Reed].

To Clothe the Naked and Two Other Plays. Trans. William Murray. New York: Dutton; Toronto: Irwin, 1962. [*The Rules of the Game, The Pleasure of Honesty*].

Tonight We Improvise. Trans. Samuel Putnam. New York: Dutton, 1932, 1938; trans. Marta Abba. New York: Samuel French, [1960].

The Wives' Friend. Trans. Marta Abba. New York: Samuel French, [1959].

NOVELS

The Late Mattia Pascal. Trans. Arthur Livingston. London: Dent, 1923; New York: Dutton, 1923, 1934. Trans. William Weaver. New York: Doubleday, 1964; Los Angeles: Eridanos, 1988.

The Old and the Young. Trans. C.K. Scott Moncrieff. New York: Dutton, 1928, 1933; London: Chatto & Windus, 1928, 1930.

One, No One, One Hundred Thousand. Trans. Samuel Putnam. New York: Dutton, 1933.

The Outcast. Trans. Leo Ongley. New York: Dutton, 1925, 1935; London: Dent, 1925.

Shoot: The Notebooks of Serafino Gubbio Cinematograph Operator. Trans. C.K. Scott Moncrieff. New York: Dutton, 1926, 1934; London: Chatto & Windus, 1927, 1930.

SHORT STORIES

Better Think Twice About It and Twelve Other Stories. Trans. Arthur and Henrie Mayne. London: Lane, 1933, 1940; New York: Dutton, 1934, 1935.

'The Blessing,' 'The Starling and the Angel One Hundred and One.' Trans. F.M. Guercio, in *Anthology of Contemporary Italian Prose.* London: Scholastic Press, 1931.

A Character in Distress. Trans. Michele Pettina. London: Duckworth, 1938. [A collection of nineteen short stories by Pirandello; published in the United States as] *His Medals and Other Stories.* New York: Dutton, 1939.

'The Dinner Guest.' Trans. anon. *The Golden Book* (July 1934).

'Diploma.' Trans. J. Redfern. *The Forthnightly Review* (July 1939).

'A Dream of Christmas.' Trans. Frederick May. Leeds: The Pirandello Society, 1959.

'A Finch, a Cat, and the Stars.' Trans. J. Redfern. *The Listener* (Sept. 1934).

'Fly.' Trans. R. Wellman. *The Forum* (24 Feb. 1924).

'Goy.' Trans. Arthur Livingston. *Menorah Journal* (Feb. 1924).

'Here's Another!' Trans. J. Redfern. *The Forthnightly Review* (Nov. 1933).

The Horse in the Moon: Twelve Short Stories. Trans. Samuel Putnam. New York: Dutton, 1932.

'Mere Formality.' Trans. anon. *The Golden Book* (Sept. 1925).

The Merry Go Round of Love and Selected Stories. Trans. Frances Keene and Lily Duplaix. New York: NAL, 1964.

'The Miracle of Two Bears.' Trans. anon. *Living Age* (30 Jan. 1936).

'Miss Holloway's Goat.' Trans. J. Redfern. *The Golden Book* (May 1934). [Also published as] 'The Little Black Kid.' *The Listener* (21 Nov. 1934).

The Naked Truth and Eleven Other Stories. Trans. Arthur and Henrie Mayne. New York: Dutton, 1934; London: Lane, 1934, 1940, 1947.

'Portrait.' Trans. anon. *Living Age* (1 Nov. 1929).

'Reserved Coffin.' Trans. J. Harry. *The Golden Book* (Jan. 1926).

'Shoes at the Door.' Trans. anon. *Living Age* (15 Nov. 1924).

Short Stories. Trans. Lily Duplaix. New York: Simon & Schuster, 1959.

Short Stories. Trans. Frederick May. New York: Oxford Univ. Press, 1964; London: Oxford Univ. Press, 1965.

'Sicilian Limes.' Trans. anon. *The Golden Book* (Jan. 1934).

'The Starling and the Angel One Hundred and One.' Trans. F.M. Guercio. *The Berdsmondsey Book* (June 1927).

'Through the Other Wife's Eyes.' Trans. J. Redfern. *The Forthnightly Review* (April 1933). [Also published as] 'With Other Eyes,' in *The Armchair Esquire.* New York: Putnam's Sons, 1958.

'To the Hoe.' Trans. Ben Johnson, in *Stories of Modern Italy.* New York: The Modern Library, 1960.

'The Tragedy of a Character,' *The Rodestone*, 38, 2 (1946).

'Truth.' Trans. J. Redfern. *The Forthnightly Review* (June 1934).

'Two Double Beds.' Trans. anon. *The Spectator* (24 Nov. 1933).

Major Criticism on Pirandello

Bentley, Eric R. 'Il tragico imperatore,' *Tulane Drama Review*, 10, 3 (April 1966): 60–75.

- 'Pirandello: Joy and Torment,' in *In Search of Theater*. New York: Knopf, 1953.
- *The Playwright as Thinker: A Study of Drama in Modern Times*. New York: Harcourt, Brace & World, 1967.
- *Theater of War*. New York: Viking, 1973.

Biasin, Gian Paolo, and Manuela Gieri, eds. *Luigi Pirandello. Contemporary Perspectives*. Toronto: Univ. of Toronto Press, 1999.

Bishop, Thomas. *Pirandello and the French Theater*. New York: NYU Press, 1960.

Brose, Margaret. 'Structures of Ambiguity in Pirandello's *Liolà*,' *Yale Italian Studies*, 2, 3 (Spring 1978): 115–41.

Brustein, Robert S. 'Luigi Pirandello,' in *The Theater of Revolt. An Approach to Modern Drama*. Boston: Little Brown, 1964. 279–317.
- *Seasons of Discontent: Dramatic Opinions 1959–1965*. New York: Simon & Schuster, 1965.

Büdel, Oscar. *Pirandello*. New York: Hillary House, 1966; London: Bowes & Bowes, 1966.

Cambon, Glauco, ed. *Pirandello: A Collection of Critical Essays*. Englewood Cliffs, NJ: Prentice Hall, 1967.

Caputi, Anthony. *Pirandello and the Crisis of Modern Consciousness*. Urbana: Urbana Univ. Press, 1988.

Caute, David. *The Illusion: An Essay on Politics, Theater, and the Novel*. New York: Harper & Row, 1972.

Chiaramonte, Nicola. 'Pirandello and Humor,' in *The Worm of Consciousness and Other Essays*. New York: Harcourt, 1976. 80–3.

Corrigan, Beatrice. 'Pirandello and the Theater of the Absurd,' *Cesare Barbieri Courier*, 8, 1 (1961).

Di Gaetani, John L., ed. *A Companion to Pirandello Studies*. Westport, CT: Greenwood Press, 1990.

Dombroski, Robert S. 'Laudisi's Laughter and the Social Dimension of *Right You Are (If You Think So)*,' *Modern Drama*, 16 (1973): 337–64.

Dukore, Bernard F., and Daniel C. Gerould. 'Explosions and Implosions: Avant-Garde Drama between World Wars,' *Educational Theater Journal*, 21 (1969): 1–16.

Esslin, Martin. 'Pirandello: Master of the Naked Masks,' in *Reflections: Essays on Modern Theater*. New York: Doubleday, 1969. [Also in *Brief Chronicles: Essays of Modern Theatre*. London: Temple Smith, 1970. 59–67].

Feng, Carol B. 'Reconciliation of Movement and Form in *Diana e la Tuda*,' *Modern Drama*, 10, 4 (1968): 410–15.

Gieri, Manuela. *Contemporary Italian Filmmaking. Strategies of Subversion. Piran-*

dello, Fellini, Scola, and the Directors of the New Generation. Toronto: Univ. of Toronto Press, 1995.

Gilman, Richard. *The Making of Modern Drama*. New York: Farrar, Straus, 1974.

Giudice, Gaspare. *Pirandello. A Biography*. London: Oxford Univ. Press, 1975.

Gordon, Jan B. '*Sei personaggi in cerca d'autore:* Myth, Ritual, and Pirandello's Anti-Symbolist Theater,' *Forum Italicum*, 6 (1972): 333–55.

Gunzberg, Maggie. *Patriarchal Representations. Gender and Discourse in Pirandello's Theater*. Oxford: Berg, 1994.

Heffner, Hubert C. 'Pirandello and the Nature of Man,' in *Modern Drama: Essays in Criticism*. Ed. Travis Bogard and William Oliver. New York: Oxford Univ. Press, 1965.

Hoover, Clark. 'Existentialism in Pirandello's *Sei Personaggi*,' *Italica*, 43, 3 (Sept. 1966): 276–84.

Illiano, Antonio. 'Pirandello in England and the United States: A Chronological List of Criticism,' *Bulletin of the N.Y. Public Library* (Feb. 1967).

– 'A View of the Italian Absurd from Pirandello to Eduardo De Filippo.' *Proceedings of the Comparative Literature Symposium*, 3. Lubbock, TX: Texas Tech University, 1970.

Kennedy, Andrew K. '*Six Characters*: Pirandello's Last Tape,' *Modern Drama*, 12 (1960): 1–9.

Lawrence, Kenneth. 'Luigi Pirandello: Holding Nature up to the Mirror,' *Italica*, 47 (1970): 61–77.

Loriggio, Franco. 'Life and Death: Pirandello's "Man with the Flower in His Mouth,"' *Italian Quarterly*, 47–8 (1969): 151–60.

Lucas, Frank L. *The Drama of Chekhov, Synge, Yeats, and Pirandello*. London: Cassell, 1963.

Lumley, F. 'The Mask and the Face of Luigi Pirandello,' in *New Trends in Twentieth Century Drama*. London: Oxford Univ. Press, 1967.

MacKlintock, Lander. *The Age of Pirandello*. Bloomington, IN: 1951.

Matthaei, Renate. *Luigi Pirandello*. New York: Ungar, 1973.

Mignone, Mario. 'The Theater of Pirandello and Brecht: Some Points of Contact,' *NEMLA Italian Studies*, 2 (1978): 63–85.

Moestrup, Jorn. *The Structural Pattern of Pirandello's Work*. Odense: Odense Univ. Press, 1972.

Nagy, Moses M. 'A Quest for Truth through Love and Reason: Marivaux and Pirandello,' *Review of National Literatures*, 14 (1987): 47–57.

Newberry, Wilma. *The Pirandellian Mode in Spanish Literature from Cervantes to Sastre*. Albany: State Univ. Press of New York, 1973.

Nolan, David. 'Theory in Action: Pirandello's *Sei personaggi*,' *Forum for Modern Language Studies*, 4 (1968): 269–76.

Nulf, Frank. 'Pirandello and the Cinema,' *Film Quarterly*, 24, 2 (1970): 40–8.

Oliver, Roger W. *Dreams of Passion. The Theater of Luigi Pirandello*. New York: NYU Press, 1972.

Paolucci, Anne. 'Pirandello: Experience as Expression of Will,' *Forum Italicum*, 7, 3 (1973): 404–14.

– *Pirandello's Theater. The Recovery of the Modern Stage for Dramatic Art*. Carbondale: Southern Illinois Univ. Press, 1974.

– 'Theater of Illusion: Pirandello's *Liolà* and Machiavelli's *Mandragola*,' *Comparative Literature Studies*, 9, 1 (1972): 44–57.

Poggioli, Renato. 'Pirandello in Retrospect,' *Italian Quarterly*, 1, 4 (Winter 1958): 19–47; and in *The Spirit of the Letter*. Cambridge, MA: Harvard Univ. Press, 1965.

Radcliff-Umstead, Douglas. *The Mirror of Our Anguish. A Study of Pirandello's Narrative Writings*. Madison, NJ: Farleigh Dickinson Univ. Press, 1978.

Ragusa, Olga. 'Correlated Terms in Pirandello's Conception of Umorismo,' in *The Two Hesperias*. Ed. Americo Bugliani. Madrid: Turanzas, 1978.

– *Luigi Pirandello*. Columbia Univ. Press, 1968.

– *Pirandello. An Approach to His Theater*. Edinburgh Univ. Press, 1980.

– 'Pirandello's Haunted House,' *Studies in Short Fiction*, 10 (1973): 235–42.

Ray, John B. 'A Case of Identity: The Source of Pirandello's *As You Desire Me*,' *Modern Drama*, 15 (1973): 433–9.

Soliuzzo, Richard A. 'The Use of the Mask in "The Great God Brown" and *Six Characters in Search of an Author*,' *Educational Theater Journal*, 18 (1966): 224–9.

Starkie, Walter. *Luigi Pirandello*. London: Dent, 1926; Berkeley: Univ. of California Press, 1965.

Stocchi-Perrucchio, Donatella. *Pirandello and the Vagaries of Knowledge. A Reading of* Il fu Mattia Pascal. Stanford: Anma Libri, 1991.

Stone, Jennifer. *Pirandello's Naked Prompt*. Ravenna: Longo, 1989.

Styan, J.L. *The Dark Comedy: The Development of Modern Comic Tragedy*. Cambridge: Cambridge Univ. Press, 1948.

Uwah, Godwin O. *Pirandellism and the Plays of Samuel Beckett*. Potomac, MD: Scripta Humanistica, 1991.

Vittorini, Domenico. *The Drama of Luigi Pirandello*. New York: Rusell & Russell, 1969.

William, Herman. 'Pirandello and Possibility,' *Tulane Drama Review*, 10, 3 (Spring 1966): 91–111.

Williams, Raymond. *Modern Tragedy*. Palo Alto, CA: Stanford Univ. Press, 1966.

In English and Italian

Proceedings of the Annual Meetings at the Centro Nazionale di Studi Pirandelliani

I miti di Pirandello. Ed. Enzo Lauretta. Palermo: Palumbo, 1975.
Il romanzo di Pirandello. Ed. Enzo Lauretta. Palermo: Palumbo, 1976.
Il teatro nel teatro di Pirandello. Ed. Enzo Lauretta. Agrigento: Centro Nazionale di Studi Pirandelliani, 1977.
Pirandello e il cinema. Ed. Enzo Lauretta. Agrigento: Centro Nazionale di Studi Pirandelliani, 1978.
Gli atti unici di Pirandello (tra narrativa e teatro). Ed. Stefano Milioto. Agrigento: Centro Nazionale di Studi Pirandelliani, 1978.
Le Novelle di Pirandello. Ed. Stefano Milioto. Agrigento: Centro Nazionale di Studi Pirandelliani, 1980.
Pirandello poeta. Ed. P.D. Giovanelli. Firenze: Vallecchi, 1981.
Pirandello saggista. Ed. Paola Daniela Giovanelli. Palermo: Palumbo, 1982.
Pirandello e il teatro del suo tempo. Ed. Stefano Milioto. Agrigento: Centro Nazionale di Studi Pirandelliani, 1983.
Il teatro dialettale di Pirandello. Palermo: Palumbo, 1983.
Pirandello e la cultura del suo tempo. Ed. Stefano Milioto and Paolo Scrivano. Agrigento: Centro Nazionale di Studi Pirandelliani, 1983.
Pirandello e la Germania. Ed. Gilda Pennica. Palermo: Palumbo, 1984.
Studi pirandelliani a Malta. Ed. Stefano Milioto. Palermo: Palumbo, 1985.
Pirandello e la drammaturgia tra le due guerre. Ed. Enzo Scrivano. Agrigento: Centro Nazionale di Studi Pirandelliani, 1985.
Teoria e prassi teatrale. Roma: La Nuova Italia Scientifica, 1986.
Testo e messinscena in Pirandello. Roma: La Nuova Italia Scientifica, 1986.
Lo strappo nel cielo di carta. Introduzione alla lettura del Fu Mattia Pascal. Roma: La Nuova Italia Scientifica, 1988.
La donna in Pirandello. Ed. Stefano Milioto. Agrigento: Centro Nazionale di Studi Pirandelliani, 1988.
Pirandello e D'Annunzio. Palermo: Palumbo, 1989.
La 'persona' nell'opera di Luigi Pirandello. Ed. Enzo Lauretta. Milano: Mursia, 1990.
Pirandello e l'oltre. Ed. Enzo Lauretta. Milano: Mursia, 1991.
Pirandello e la politica. Ed. Enzo Lauretta. Milano: Mursia, 1992.
Pirandello e il teatro. Ed. Enzo Lauretta. Milano: Mursia, 1993.
Pirandello e la lingua. Ed. Enzo Lauretta. Milano: Mursia, 1994.
Pirandello: teatro e cinema. Ed. Enzo Lauretta. Palermo: Palumbo, 1995.

Le Fonti di Pirandello. Ed. Antonio Alessio and Giuliana Sanguineti Katz. Palermo: Palumbo, 1996.

Proceedings of Other Meetings of Some Importance

Atti del Congresso Internazionale di Studi Pirandelliani. Firenze: Le Monnier, 1967.
Il teatro di Pirandello. Convegno di studi. Asti: Centro Nazionale di Studi Alfieriani, 1964.
Luigi Pirandello: Poetica e presenza. Ed. W. Geerts, F. Musarra, and S. Vanvolsen. Leuven-Roma: Leuven Univ. Press and Bulzoni, 1987.
Pirandello '86. Ed. G.P. Biasin and N.J. Perella. Roma: Bulzoni, 1987.
Pirandello in America. Ed. Mario Mignone. Roma: Bulzoni, 1988.

Journals of Pirandellian Studies

Pirandellian Studies
P.S.A. [The Pirandello Society of America]
Rivista di studi pirandelliani

Issues of Journals Mostly or Entirely Devoted to Pirandellian Topics (in Chronological Order)

Modern Drama, 6, 4 (Feb. 1964).
Tulane Drama Review, 10, 3 (Spring 1966).
Italica, 44, 1 (March 1967).
Forum Italicum, 1, 4 (Dec. 1967).
World Theater, 16, 3 (1967).
Il Veltro, 12, 1–2 (1968).
Italica, 52, 2 (Summer 1975).
Modern Drama, 20, 4 (1977).
Review of National Literatures, 14 (1987).
Canadian Journal of Italian Studies, 12, 38–9 (1989); 13, 40–1 (1990).

In Italian

Master Editions of Pirandello's Works

Pirandello, Luigi. *Maschere nude.* 2 vols. Milano: Mondadori, 1978.
– *Novelle per un anno.* 2 vols. Milano Mondadori, 1956–7.

– *Saggi, poesie, scritti varii*. Milano: Mondadori, 1977.
– *Tutti i romanzi*. Milano: Mondadori, 1957.

Major Criticism on Pirandello

Alonge, Roberto. *Pirandello*. Bari: Laterza, 1997.

Anderson, Gosta. *Arte e teoria. Studi sulla poetica del giovane Pirandello*. Stoccolma: Almquist & Wiksell, 1966.

Apollonio, Mario. *Attualità di Pirandello*. Milano-Roma: U.I.P.C., 1969.

Artioli, Umberto. *L'officina segreta di Pirandello*. Bari: Laterza, 1998.

Baccolo, Luigi. *Pirandello*. Milano: Bocca, 1949.

Balestra, Fernando. *Pirandello e il teatro dei problemi*. Roma: Cremonese, 1975.

Barbina, Alfredo. *Bibliografia della critica pirandelliana 1889–1961*. Firenze: Le Monnier, 1967.

Barilli, Renato. *Pirandello. Una rivoluzione culturale*. Milano: Mursia, 1986.

Bonanate, Mariapia. *Luigi Pirandello*. Torino: Borla, 1972.

Borlenghi, Aldo. *Pirandello o dell'ambiguità*. Padova: R.A.D.A.R., 1968.

Borsellino, Nino. *Ritratti e immagini di Pirandello*. Bari: Laterza, 1991.

Caioli, Ferdinando. *L'avventura di Pirandello*. Catania: Giannotta, 1969.

Calendoli, Giovanni. *Luigi Pirandello*. Roma: La Navicella, 1962.

Cantoro, Umberto. *Luigi Pirandello e il problema della personalità*. Bologna: Gallo, 1954.

Corsinovi, Gabriella. *Pirandello e l'espressionismo*. Genova: Tilgher, 1979.

– 'Rassegna pirandelliana (1973–1978),' *Otto/Novecento*, 3, 2 (1979).

Costa, Simona. *Pirandello*. Firenze: La Nuova Italia, 1978.

Crifò, Cosmo. *Il teatro di Pirandello dagli inizi all'Enrico IV*. Palermo: Manfredi, 1979.

Croce, Benedetto. 'Pirandello,' in *La letteratura della nuova Italia*, 6. Bari: Laterza 1946.

D'Amico, Sandro. *Pirandello ieri e oggi*. Milano: Quaderni del Piccolo Teatro, 1961.

De Bella, Nino. *Pirandello oggi*. Roma: Ciranna, 1970.

Di Maria, Vincenzo. *Il teatro di Pirandello*. Catania: Di Maria, 1974.

Di Sacco, Paolo. *L'epopea del personaggio. Uno studio sul teatro di Pirandello*. Roma: Lucarini, 1984.

– 'Rassegna di studi pirandelliani: gli anni Ottanta,' *Testo*, 8 (1988).

– 'Rassegna pirandelliana (1988–1993),' *Testo*, 26 (luglio–dicembre 1993).

– 'Aggiornamenti pirandelliani,' *Otto/Novecento*, 19, 1 (gennaio–febbraio, 1995).

Eco, Umberto. 'Pirandello ridens,' *Sugli specchi*. Milano: Bompiani, 1985.

Ferrante, Luigi. *Pirandello*. Firenze: Parenti, 1958.

Ferrara, Mario N. *Luigi Pirandello*. Roma: Ciranna, 1968.
Frassica, Pietro. *A Marta Abba per non morire. Sull'epistolario inedito tra Pirandello e la sua attrice*. Milano: Mursia, 1991.
Gardair, Jean-Michel. *Pirandello e il suo doppio*. Roma: Abete, 1977.
Giacalone, Giuseppe. *Luigi Pirandello*. Brescia: La Scuola, 1966.
Giudice, Gaspare. *Pirandello*. Torino: U.T.E.T., 1963.
Grignani, M.A. *Retoriche Pirandelliane*. Napoli: Liguori, 1993.
Guasco, Cesare. *Ragione e mito nell'arte di Luigi Pirandello*. Roma: Arte e Storia, 1954.
Illiano, Antonio. *Introduzione alla critica pirandelliana*. Verona: Fiorini, 1976.
– *Metapsichica e letteratura in Pirandello*. Firenze: Vallecchi, 1982.
Janner, Arminio. *Luigi Pirandello*. Firenze: La Nuova Italia, 1973.
Lauretta, Enzo. *Pirandello, umano e irreligioso*. Milano: Gastaldi, 1953.
– *Luigi Pirandello. Storia di un personaggio fuori chiave*. Milano: Mursia, 1980.
Leone De Castris, Arcangelo. *Storia di Pirandello*. Bari: Laterza, 1952, 1975.
Luperini, Romano. *Introduzione a Pirandello*. Bari: Laterza, 1992.
Mariani, Umberto. *La creazione del vero. Il maggior teatro di Pirandello*. Fiesole: Cadmo, 2001.
Mazzacurati, Giancarlo. *Pirandello nel romanzo europeo*. Bologna: Il Mulino, 1987.
Mazzali, Ettore. *Pirandello*. Firenze: La Nuova Italia, 1973.
Mirmina, Emilia. *Pirandello novelliere*. Ravenna: Longo, 1973.
Monti, Silvana. *Pirandello*. Palermo: Palumbo, 1974.
Munafò, Gaetano. *Conoscere Pirandello*. Firenze: Le Monnier, 1965, 1974.
Puglisi, Filippo. *L'arte di Luigi Pirandello*. Messina-Firenze: D'Anna, 1958.
Querci, Giovanni. *Pirandello. L'inconsistenza dell'oggettività*. Bari: Laterza, 1992.
Roffarè, Francesco T. *L'essenzialità problematica e dialettica del teatro di Pirandello*. Firenze: Le Monnier, 1972.
Salinari, Carlo. *Luigi Pirandello*. Napoli: Liguori, 1968.
Sciascia, Leonardo. *Pirandello e il pirandellismo*. Caltanisetta: Sciascia, 1953.
Scrivano, Riccardo. *La vocazione contesa. Note su Pirandello e il teatro*. Roma: Bulzoni, 1987.
Tilgher, Adriano. 'Il teatro di Luigi Pirandello,' in *Studi sul teatro contemporaneo*. Roma: Libreria di Scienze e di Lettere, 1923. 157–218.
Vicentini, Claudio. *L'estetica di Pirandello*. Milano: Mursia, 1970.
– *Pirandello. Il disagio del teatro*. Venezia: Marsilio, 1993.
Virdia, Ferdinando. *Invito alla lettura di Pirandello*. Milano: Mursia, 1976.
Zangrilli, Franco. *L'arte novellistica di Pirandello*. Ravenna: Longo, 1983.
– *Linea pirandelliana nella narrativa contemporanea*. Ravenna: Longo, 1990.
– *Pirandello e i classici. Da Euripide a Verga*. Firenze: Cadmo, 1995.
– *Le sorprese dell'intertestualità: Cervantes e Pirandello*. Torino: S.E.I., 1996.

Index